THE HEAVENLY

CITY OF THE

EIGHTEENTH-CENTURY

PHILOSOPHERS

BASED ON THE STORRS LECTURES

DELIVERED AT YALE UNIVERSITY

THE HEAVENLY
CITY OF THE
EIGHTEENTH-CENTURY
PHILOSOPHERS

BY CARL L. BECKER

NEW HAVEN & LONDON
YALE UNIVERSITY PRESS

Printed in the United States of America by
BookCrafters, Inc., Fredericksburg, Virginia.

ISBN: 0–300–00297–1 (cloth),
        0–300–00017–0 (paper)

54 53 52 51 50 49 48

Preface

THIS *small volume contains four lectures delivered in the School of Law in Yale University, on the Storrs Foundation, late in the month of April, 1931. In preparing the lectures for the press, I have made a few changes, mainly verbal; but certain passages in the last three lectures as here printed were necessarily, for lack of time, omitted when the lectures were delivered.*

For many courtesies extended to me at the time the lectures were given, I am indebted to the members of the faculty and to the students in the School of Law, and in the Department of History, Yale University.

C. B.

Ithaca, New York,
May, 1932.

Contents

THE HEAVENLY CITY

I

Climates of Opinion

> Superstition, like many other fancies, very easily
> loses its power when, instead of flattering our
> vanity, it stands in the way of it. GOETHE.

I

LIKE most men I hold certain cherished beliefs which
I think valid because they follow logically from
known and obvious facts. It often distresses me to
find that an intimate friend of mine rejects one or
other of these beliefs, even after I have laid before
him all the relevant facts and have repeatedly re-
traced for his benefit the logical steps that ought to
convince a reasonable mind. It may happen (is almost sure to, in fact) that he cannot refute my argument. No matter. Convinced against his will, he is of
the same opinion still; and I realize at last that his
mind is, unfortunately, not entirely open. Some perverse emotion, some deep-seated prejudice or unexamined preconception blinds him to the truth.

The disturbing prejudice which leads my friend to
wrong conclusions I readily forgive because I understand it. It is a minor error into which I myself, but
for the grace of some happy chance, might have
fallen. In major matters we agree well enough, for it

happens that we are both professors. Our experience and our interests are much the same. The facts that appear relevant and the deductions that win assent are, generally speaking, the same for him as for me. Most of our premises, and the phrases we employ without analysis, are those familiar in the schools. Agreeing so well in fundamentals, we may argue copiously throughout the night, except in opinion, as Carlyle said, not being divided.

It is less easy for us, two professors, to argue throughout the night with men of another way of life—with, let us say, politicians or preachers. The argument soon falters for want of agreement. Facts which they accept as relevant we question or regard as negligible. Processes of reasoning which bring conviction to us they dismiss with perverse and casual levity as academic. Before the night is well begun the discussion peters out. We see that it is useless to go on because their thought is vitiated, not merely on the surface by prejudices peculiar to them as individuals, but fundamentally by unconscious preconceptions that are common to all men of their profession.

Nevertheless, great as our differences are, all of us —professors, politicians, preachers—would no doubt find that we had much in common after all if it were possible to meet in the flesh some distinguished representatives of a former age. Let us for the moment give way to fantasy and suppose that we could, by rubbing a Mazda lamp, bring Dante and Thomas Aquinas before us. Since it would be a waste of precious time to discuss the weather, we might ask St. Thomas to define for us the concept of natural law, a phrase as much used in his time as it is in ours. Always apt at definition, St. Thomas would not hesitate. He would say:

Since all things subject to Divine providence are ruled and measured by the eternal law . . .; it is evident that all things partake somewhat of the eternal law, in so far as, namely, from its being imprinted on them, they derive their respective inclinations to their proper acts and ends. Now among all others, the rational creature is subject to Divine providence in the most excellent way, in so far as it partakes of a share of providence, by being provident both for itself and for others. Wherefore it has a share of the Eternal Reason, whereby it has a natural inclination to its proper act and end: and this participation of the eternal law in the rational creature is called the natural law.[1]

Having listened to this concise definition we might decide that after all a less academic subject would be better, for example, the League of Nations, something on which Dante had much to say under the caption of *De monarchia*. Being in favor of the League, Dante might support his position by the following argument:

Mankind is a whole with relation to certain parts, and

[1] *Summa theologica,* Part II (First Part), Q. XCI, art. ii.

is a part with relation to a certain whole. It is a whole, of course, with relation to particular kingdoms and nations, as was shown above, and it is a part with relation to the whole universe, as is self-evident. Therefore, in the manner in which the constituent parts of . . . humanity correspond to humanity as a whole, so, we say, . . . humanity corresponds as a part to its larger whole. That the constituent parts of . . . humanity correspond to humanity as a whole through the one only principle of submission to a single Prince, can be easily gathered from what has gone before. And therefore humanity corresponds to the universe itself, or to its Prince, who is God, . . . simply through one only principle, namely, the submission to a single Prince. We conclude from this that Monarchy [League of Nations] is necessary to the world for its well-being.[2]

After this the discussion would no doubt drag heavily. For what could any of us say in reply to either Dante or St. Thomas? Whatever we might say, on one side or the other, it is unlikely that either of them would find it strictly relevant, or even understand which side of the argument we were espousing. One thing only would be clear to us, namely, that the two men employed the same technique for achieving obscurity. Perhaps our first impulse would be to concede charitably that the distinguished guests were not at their best; our second, to mutter that, with all due respect, they were paying us with nonsensical rigmaroles. It may be so; to the modern

[2] *De monarchia* (English ed., 1904), Bk. I, chap. vii, pp. 24–25.

mind, indeed, it is so; and it would clearly be un-
wise, for example, to reprint the *De monarchia* as a
League of Nations propagandist tract. Nevertheless,
what troubles me is that I cannot dismiss Dante or
St. Thomas as unintelligent men. The judgment of
posterity has placed them among the lordly ones of
the earth; and if their arguments are unintelligible
to us the fact cannot be attributed to lack of intelligence in them. They were at least as intelligent and
learned as many who in our time have argued for or
against the League of Nations—as intelligent perhaps as Clémenceau, as learned as Wilson.

Professor Whitehead has recently restored to cir-
culation a seventeenth-century phrase—"climate of
opinion." The phrase is much needed. Whether arguments command assent or not depends less upon the
logic that conveys them than upon the climate of
opinion in which they are sustained. What renders
Dante's argument or St. Thomas' definition meaningless to us is not bad logic or want of intelligence,
but the medieval climate of opinion—those instinctively held preconceptions in the broad sense, that
Weltanschauung or world pattern—which imposed
upon Dante and St. Thomas a peculiar use of the
intelligence and a special type of logic. To understand why we cannot easily follow Dante or St.
Thomas it is necessary to understand (as well as may
be) the nature of this climate of opinion.

It is well known that the medieval world pattern,

deriving from Greek logic and the Christian story, was fashioned by the church which for centuries imposed its authority upon the isolated and anarchic society of western Europe. The modern mind, which curiously notes and carefully describes everything, can indeed describe this climate of opinion although it cannot live in it. In this climate of opinion it was an unquestioned fact that the world and man in it had been created in six days by God the Father, an omniscient and benevolent intelligence, for an ultimate if inscrutable purpose. Although created perfect, man had through disobedience fallen from grace into sin and error, thereby incurring the penalty of eternal damnation. Yet happily a way of atonement and salvation had been provided through the propitiatory sacrifice of God's only begotten son. Helpless in themselves to avert the just wrath of God, men were yet to be permitted, through his mercy, and by humility and obedience to his will, to obtain pardon for sin and error. Life on earth was but a means to this desired end, a temporary probation for the testing of God's children. In God's appointed time, the Earthly City would come to an end, the earth itself be swallowed up in flames. On that last day good and evil men would be finally separated. For the recalcitrant there was reserved a place of everlasting punishment; but the faithful would be gathered with God in the Heavenly City, there in perfection and felicity to dwell forever.

Existence was thus regarded by the medieval man as a cosmic drama, composed by the master dramatist according to a central theme and on a rational plan. Finished in idea before it was enacted in fact, before the world began written down to the last syllable of recorded time, the drama was unalterable either for good or evil. There it was, precisely defined, to be understood as far as might be, but at all events to be remorselessly played out to its appointed end. The duty of man was to accept the drama as written, since he could not alter it; his function, to play the rôle assigned. That he might play his rôle according to the divine text, subordinate authorities —church and state—deriving their just powers from the will of God, were instituted among men to dispose them to submission and to instruct them in their proper lines. Intelligence was essential, since God had endowed men with it. But the function of intelligence was strictly limited. Useless to inquire curiously into the origin or final state of existence, since both had been divinely determined and sufficiently revealed. Useless, even impious, to inquire into its ultimate meaning, since God alone could fully understand it. The function of intelligence was therefore to demonstrate the truth of revealed knowledge, to reconcile diverse and pragmatic experience with the rational pattern of the world as given in faith.

Under the bracing influence of this climate of opinion the best thought of the time assumed a thor-

7

oughly rationalistic form. I know it is the custom to call the thirteenth century an age of faith, and to contrast it with the eighteenth century, which is thought to be preëminently the age of reason. In a sense the distinction is true enough, for the word "reason," like other words, has many meanings. Since eighteenth-century writers employed reason to discredit Christian dogma, a "rationalist" in common parlance came to mean an "unbeliever," one who denied the truth of Christianity. In this sense Voltaire was a rationalist, St. Thomas a man of faith. But this use of the word is unfortunate, since it obscures the fact that reason may be employed to support faith as well as to destroy it. There were, certainly, many differences between Voltaire and St. Thomas, but the two men had much in common for all that. What they had in common was the profound conviction that their beliefs could be reasonably demonstrated. In a very real sense it may be said of the eighteenth century that it was an age of faith as well as of reason, and of the thirteenth century that it was an age of reason as well as of faith.

This is not a paradox. On the contrary, passionate faith and an expert rationalism are apt to be united. Most men (of course I need parentheses here to take care of simple-minded folk and the genuine mystics)—most intelligent men who believe passionately that God's in his heaven and all's right with the world—feel the need of good and sufficient reasons

8

for their faith, all the more so if a few disturbing doubts have crept in to make them uneasy. This is perhaps one of the reasons why the thought of Dante's time was so remorselessly rationalistic. The faith was still intact, surely; but it was just ceasing to be instinctively held—its ablest adherents just becoming conscious that it was held as faith. All the more need, therefore, for proving it up to the hilt. It was precisely because St. Thomas believed in a divinely ordered world that he needed, for his own peace of mind, an impregnable rational proof of a divinely ordered world. He could never have said, with Tertullian, "I believe that which is absurd." He could easily have said, with St. Anselm, "I believe in order that I may know." He might well have added, "I should be distressed indeed if I could not find a rational demonstration of what I know."

To reconcile diverse and pragmatic experience with a rational pattern of the world is a sufficiently difficult task, even if experience be limited and knowledge not too great—an impossible task unless logic proves amenable to the reasons of the heart which reason knows not of. And so the men of Dante's time found it. To devise a highly intricate dialectic was, of course, essential, but the least of their difficulties; for even with the aid of Aristotle's logic it was still not always possible to press what William James called the "irreducible brute facts" into the neat categories prescribed by the faith. It was therefore necessary, in emergencies, to seek, beneath the literal significance of authoritative texts, hidden meanings which could be elicited only by the aid of a symbolical interpretation. *Litera gesta docet; quid credas, allegoria; moralis quid agas; quo tendas, anagogia*—so runs the famous formula which the schoolmen devised for use in the schools, a formula which might be freely rendered:

> The letter teaches what we know,
> Anagogia what we hope is so;
> Faith's confirmed by allegories,
> Conduct's shaped by moral stories.

Thus it was possible for the thirteenth century, employing a highly intricate dialectic supported on occasion by a symbolical interpretation, to justify the ways of God to man. Paradise lost and paradise regained—such was the theme of the drama of existence as understood in that age; and all the best minds of the time were devoted to its explication. Theology related and expounded the history of the world. Philosophy was the science that rationalized and reconciled nature and history. Logic provided both theology and philosophy with an adequate methodology. As a result we have, among innumerable other works, the *Summa theologica,* surely one of the most amazing and stupendous products of the human mind. It is safe to say that never before or since has the wide world been so neatly boxed and

compassed, so completely and confidently understood, every known detail of it fitted, with such subtle and loving precision, into a consistent and convincing whole.

We have now remained in the medieval climate of
opinion as long as it is perhaps quite safe to do. Let
us then descend from the peaks of the thirteenth to
the lower levels of the twentieth century—to an atmosphere in which, since it is charged with a richer
factual content, we can breathe with greater ease and
comfort.

II

What then can we—scientists, historians, philosophers of the twentieth century—make of the the-
ology-history, the philosophy-science, the dialectic-
methodology of the thirteenth century? We can
—must, indeed, since that is our habit—peruse with
infinite attention and indifference the serried, weighty
folios of the *Summa* and such works now carefully
preserved in libraries. We can perhaps wonder a little—although, since nothing is alien to us, we are
rarely caught wondering—at the unfailing zest, the
infinite patience, the extraordinary ingenuity and
acumen therein displayed. We can even understand
what is therein recorded well enough to translate it
clumsily into modern terms. The one thing we cannot do with the *Summa* of St. Thomas is to meet its
arguments on their own ground. We can neither as-

sent to them nor refute them. It does not even occur to us to make the effort, since we instinctively feel that in the climate of opinion which sustains such arguments we could only gasp for breath. Its conclusions seem to us neither true nor false, but only irrelevant; and they seem irrelevant because the world pattern into which they are so dexterously woven is no longer capable of eliciting from us either an emotional or an aesthetic response.

With the best will in the world it is quite impossible for us to conceive of existence as a divinely ordered drama, the beginning and end of which is known, the significance of which has once for all been revealed. For good or ill we must regard the world as a continuous flux, a ceaseless and infinitely complicated process of waste and repair, so that "all things and principles of things" are to be regarded as no more than "inconstant modes or fashions," as the "concurrence, renewed from moment to moment, of forces parting sooner or later on their way." The beginning of this continuous process of change is shrouded in impenetrable mist; the end seems more certain, but even less engaging. According to J. H. Jeans:

Everything points with overwhelming force to a definite event, or series of events, of creation at some time or times, not infinitely remote. The universe cannot have originated by chance out of its present ingredients, and neither can it have been always the same as now. For in either of these events no atoms would be left save such as are incapable of dissolving into radiation; there would be neither sunlight nor starlight but only a cool glow of radiation uniformly diffused through space. This is, indeed, so far as present-day science can see, the final end towards which all creation moves, and at which it must at long last arrive.[3]

We need not, of course, make immediate preparation for that far-off, portentous event; the universe is still a going concern and will outlast our time. But we may be reasonably curious about the relation of man to this inevitable running down of the universe. How did man enter this galley, and what is he doing in it? According to Professor Dampier-Whetham, science offers two possible answers:

Life . . . may be regarded either as a negligible accident in a bye-product of the cosmic process, or as the supreme manifestation of the high effort of creative evolution, for which the Earth alone, in the chances of time and space, has given a fitting home.[4]

Between these alternatives there is little enough to choose, since in either case man must be regarded as part of the cosmic process, fated to extinction with it. Let us listen to Bertrand Russell:

That man is the product of causes which had no prevision of the end they were achieving; that his origin, his

[3] *Eos, or the Wider Aspects of Cosmogony*, p. 55; quoted in Dampier-Whetham, *A History of Science*, p. 483.
[4] *A History of Science*, p. 482.

growth, his hopes and fears, his loves and his beliefs, are
but the outcome of accidental collocations of atoms; that
no fire, no heroism, no intensity of thought and feeling
can preserve an individual life beyond the grave; that all
the labours of all the ages, all the devotion, all the inspiration, all the noonday brightness of human genius are
destined to extinction in the vast death of the solar system, and that the whole temple of man's achievement
must inevitably be buried beneath the debris of a universe in ruins—all these things, if not quite beyond dis-
pute, are yet so nearly certain that no philosophy which
rejects them can hope to stand.[5]

Edit and interpret the conclusions of modern science as tenderly as we like, it is still quite impossible
for us to regard man as the child of God for whom
the earth was created as a temporary habitation.
Rather must we regard him as little more than a
chance deposit on the surface of the world, care-
lessly thrown up between two ice ages by the same
forces that rust iron and ripen corn, a sentient organism endowed by some happy or unhappy accident with intelligence indeed, but with an intelligence that is conditioned by the very forces that it
seeks to understand and to control. The ultimate
cause of this cosmic process of which man is a part,
whether God or electricity or a "stress in the ether,"
we know not. Whatever it may be, if indeed it be
anything more than a necessary postulate of thought,

[5] *Mysticism and Logic*, p. 47; quoted in Dampier-Whetham,
A History of Science, p. 487.

it appears in its effects as neither benevolent nor malevolent, as neither kind nor unkind, but merely as indifferent to us. What is man that the electron should be mindful of him! Man is but a foundling in the cosmos, abandoned by the forces that created him. Unparented, unassisted and undirected by omniscient or benevolent authority, he must fend for himself, and with the aid of his own limited intelligence find his way about in an indifferent universe.

Such is the world pattern that determines the character and direction of modern thinking. The pattern has been a long time in the weaving. It has taken eight centuries to replace the conception of existence as divinely composed and purposeful drama by the conception of existence as a blindly running flux of disintegrating energy. But there are signs that the substitution is now fully accomplished; and if we wished to reduce eight centuries of intellectual history to an epigram, we could not do better than to borrow the words of Aristophanes, "Whirl is king, having deposed Zeus."

Perhaps the most important consequence of this revolution is that we look about in vain for any semblance of the old authority, the old absolute, for any stable foothold from which to get a running start. Zeus, having been deposed, can no longer serve as a first premise of thought. It is true we may still believe in Zeus; many people do. Even scientists, historians, philosophers still accord him the customary

worship. But this is no more than a personal privi-
lege, to be exercised in private, as formerly, in Protestant countries, Papists were sometimes permitted
to celebrate mass in private chapels. No serious
scholar would now postulate the existence and goodness of God as a point of departure for explaining
the quantum theory or the French Revolution. If I
should venture, as certain historians once did, to ex-
pound the thought of the eighteenth century as having been foreordained by God for the punishment of
a perverse and stiff-necked generation, you would
shift uneasily in your chairs, you would "register"
embarrassment, and even blush a little to think that
a trusted colleague should exhibit such bad taste.
The fact is that we have no first premise. Since
Whirl is king, we must start with the whirl, the mess
of things as presented in experience. We start with
the irreducible brute fact, and we must take it as we
find it, since it is no longer permitted to coax or ca-
jole it, hoping to fit it into some or other category of
thought on the assumption that the pattern of the
world is a logical one. Accepting the fact as given,
we observe it, experiment with it, verify it, classify
it, measure it if possible, and reason about it as little as may be. The questions we ask are "What?"
and "How?" What are the facts and how are they
related? If sometimes, in a moment of absent-mind-
edness or idle diversion, we ask the question "Why?"
the answer escapes us. Our supreme object is to

measure and master the world rather than to understand it.

Since our supreme object is to measure and master the world, we can make relatively little use of theology, philosophy, and deductive logic—the three stately entrance ways to knowledge erected in the Middle Ages. In the course of eight centuries these disciplines have fallen from their high estate, and in their place we have enthroned history, science, and the technique of observation and measurement. Theology, or something that goes under that name, is still kept alive by the faithful, but only by artificial respiration. Its functions, the services it rendered in the time of St. Thomas, have been taken over, not as is often supposed by philosophy, but by history—the study of man and his world in the time sequence. Theology in the thirteenth century presented the story of man and the world according to the divine plan of salvation. It provided the men of that age with an authentic philosophy of history, and they could afford to ignore the factual experience of mankind since they were so well assured of its ultimate cause and significance. But in the succeeding centuries men turned more and more to an investigation of the recorded story of mankind, bringing to that enterprise a remarkable attention to detail, an ever greater preoccupation with the factual event. In the light of the mass of irreducible brute facts thus accumulated, the theological vision of man and his world faded into a pale replica of the original picture. In the eighteenth century the clear-cut theological philosophy of history had degenerated into an amiable and gentlemanly "philosophy teaching by example." In the early nineteenth century, history could still be regarded as the Transcendent Idea realizing itself in the actual. In our time, history is nothing but history, the notation of what has occurred, just as it happened. The object of history, according to Santayana, is quite simply "to fix the order of events throughout past times in all places." No respectable historian any longer harbors ulterior motives; and one who should surreptitiously introduce the gloss of a transcendent interpretation into the human story would deserve to be called a philosopher and straightway lose his reputation as a scholar.

I am, of course, using the word "history" in the broad sense. It is to be understood as a method of approach rather than as a special field of study. Literature and language, government and law, economics, science and mathematics, love and sport—what is there that has not in our time been studied historically? Much of what is called science is properly history, the history of biological or physical phenomena. The geologist gives us the history of the earth; the botanist relates the life history of plants. Professor Whitehead has recently illuminated physics by tracing the history of physical concepts. To regard all things in their historical setting appears, indeed, to be an instructive procedure of the modern mind. We do it without thinking, because we can scarcely think at all without doing it. The modern climate of opinion is such that we cannot seemingly understand our world unless we regard it as a going concern. We cannot properly know things as they are unless we know "how they came to be what they are." Nor is it merely, or chiefly, the succession of external events that engages our attention. No doubt St. Thomas was aware that one thing follows another. What is peculiar to the modern mind is the disposition and the determination to regard ideas and concepts, the truth of things as well as the things themselves, as changing entities, the character and significance of which at any given time can be fully grasped only by regarding them as points in an endless process of differentiation, of unfolding, of waste and repair. Let St. Thomas ask *us* to define anything—for example, the natural law—let him ask us to tell him what it *is*. We cannot do it. But, given time enough, we can relate for him its history. We can tell him what varied forms the natural law has assumed up to now. Historical-mindedness is so much a preconception of modern thought that we can identify a particular thing only by pointing to the various things it successively was before it became that particular thing which it will presently cease to be.

19

Besides the historical approach to knowledge we have another to which we are even more committed —the scientific. As history has gradually replaced theology, so science has replaced philosophy. Philosophy, it is true, has managed, much better than theology, to keep up appearances in the modern world, and at the present moment signs are not wanting of refurbishings going on in its ancient and somewhat dilapidated dwelling. Yet, it is obvious that the undisputed sway which it formerly exercised has long been usurped by natural science. In the hands of St. Thomas, philosophy, with "deductive" logic as its instrument of precision, was a method of building a rational world, its aim being to reconcile experience with revealed truth. But the influences which disposed succeeding generations to examine the facts of human history, induced them also to examine the facts of natural phenomena. The rise of history and of science were but two results of a single impulse, two aspects of the trend of modern thought away from an overdone rationalization of the facts to a more careful and disinterested examination of the facts themselves.

Galileo, for example (not that he was the first by any means), did not ask what Aristotle had said about falling bodies, or whether it was reasonable to suppose that a ten-pound weight would fall to the ground more quickly than a one-pound weight. He applied to this problem the scientific method. He dropped two weights, differing as ten to one, from the leaning tower, and noted the fact that both weights reached the ground at the same time. In such a world as this, he said in effect, this is the way falling bodies behave. If that is not possible in a rational world, then the world we live in is not a rational one. Facts are primary and what chiefly concern us; they are stubborn and irreducible and we cannot get around them. They may be in accord with reason, let us hope that they are; but whether they are so or not is only a question of fact to be determined like any other.

This subtle shift in the point of view was perhaps the most important event in the intellectual history of modern times, but its implications were not at once understood. Philosophy continued to reign, and when in the eighteenth century she added a new word to her title (calling herself natural philosophy), no one noted the fact as ominous. Galileo and his successors were philosophers too, preëminently so, since their marvelous discoveries, based upon observation and experiment, uncovered so many secret places in the world, and by promising to banish mystery from the universe seemed to leave it more obviously rational than they found it. The laws of nature and nature's God appeared henceforth to be one and the same thing, and since every part of God's handiwork could all in good time be reasonably demonstrated, the intelligent man could very well do with a minimum of faith—except, of course (the exception was tremendous but scarcely noticed at the time), faith in the uniform behavior of nature and in the capacity of reason to discover its *modus operandi.*

In the course of the nineteenth century this optimistic outlook became overcast. The marriage of fact and reason, of science and the universal laws of nature, proved to be somewhat irksome, and in the twentieth century it was, not without distress, altogether dissolved. Natural philosophy was transformed into natural science. Natural science became science, and scientists rejected, as a personal affront, the title of philosopher, which formerly they had been proud to bear. The vision of man and his world as a neat and efficient machine, designed by an intelligent Author of the Universe, gradually faded away. Professors of science ceased to speak with any assurance of the laws of nature, and were content to pursue, with unabated ardor, but without any teleological implications whatever, their proper business of observing and experimenting with the something which is the stuff of the universe, of measuring and mastering its stress and movement. "Science," said Lloyd Morgan, "deals exclusively with changes of configuration, and traces the accelerations which are observed to occur, leaving to metaphysics to deal with the underlying agency, if it exist."[6]

It is well known that the result of pursuing this

[6] *Interpretation of Nature,* p. 58.

restricted aim (the scientific method reduced to its lowest terms) has been astounding. It is needless to say that we live in a machine age, that the art of inventing is the greatest of our inventions, or that within a brief space of fifty years the outward conditions of life have been transformed. It is less well understood that this bewildering experience has given a new slant to our minds. Fresh discoveries and new inventions are no longer the result of fortunate accidents which we are expected to note with awe. They are all a part of the day's work, anticipated, deliberately intended, and brought to pass according to schedule. Novelty has ceased to excite wonder because it has ceased to be novelty; on the contrary, the strange, so habituated have we become to it, is of the very essence of the customary. There is nothing new in heaven or earth not dreamt of in our laboratories; and we should be amazed indeed if tomorrow and tomorrow and tomorrow failed to offer us something new to challenge our capacity for readjustment. Science has taught us the futility of troubling to understand the "underlying agency" of the things we use. We have found that we can drive an automobile without knowing how the carburetor works, and listen to a radio without mastering the secret of radiation. We really haven't time to stand amazed, either at the starry firmament above or the Freudian complexes within us. The multiplicity of things to manipulate and make use of so fully engages our attention that we have neither the leisure nor the inclination to seek a rational explanation of the force that makes them function so efficiently.

In dismissing the underlying agency with a casual shrug, we are in good company. The high priest of science, even more than the common man, is a past master of this art. It is one of the engaging ironies of modern thought that the scientific method, which it was once fondly hoped would banish mystery from the world, leaves it every day more inexplicable. Physics, which it was thought had dispensed with the need of metaphysics, has been transformed by its own proper researches into the most metaphysical of disciplines. The more attentively the physicist looks at the material stuff of the world the less there is to see. Under his expert treatment the substantial world of Newtonian physics has been dissolved into a complex of radiant energies. No efficient engineer or Prime Mover could have designed the world, since it can no longer be fully understood in terms of mechanics. "What is the sense of talking about a mechanical explanation," asks Professor Whitehead, "when you do not know what you mean by mechanics?"[7] We are told that if we ascribe position to anything it ceases to have determinable velocity; if we ascertain its velocity it ceases to have determinable position. The universe is said to be composed of atoms, an atom is said to be composed of a nucleus

[7] *Science and the Modern World,* p. 24.

around which electrons revolve in determinable orbits; but experiments seem to show that an electron may, for reasons best known to itself, be moving in two orbits at the same time. To this point Galileo's common-sense method of noting the behavior of things, of sticking close to the observable facts, has brought us: it has at last presented us with a fact that common sense repudiates.

What can we do? Reason and logic cry out in pain no doubt; but we have long since learned not to bother overmuch with reason and logic. Logic was formerly visualized as something outside us, something existing independently which, if we were willing, could take us by the hand and lead us into the paths of truth. We now suspect that it is something the mind has created to conceal its timidity and keep up its courage, a hocus-pocus designed to give formal validity to conclusions we are willing to accept if everybody else in our set will too. If all men are mortal (an assumption), and if Socrates was a man (in the sense assumed), no doubt Socrates must have been mortal; but we suspect that we somehow knew all this before it was submitted to the test of a syllogism. Logics have a way of multiplying in response to the changes in point of view. First there was one logic, then there were two, then there were several; so that now, according to one authority (if a contributor to the *Encyclopaedia Britannica* who ventures to employ humor can be an authority), the state of logic is "that of Israel under the Judges, every man doeth that which is right in his own eyes." With all due allowance made for mathematical logic (which has to do with concepts, not with facts), and for the logic of probability (which Mr. Keynes assures us has a probable validity), the secure foundations of deductive and inductive logic have been battered to pieces by the ascertainable facts, so that we really have no choice; we must cling to the ascertainable facts though they slay us.

Physicists, therefore, stick to the ascertainable facts. If logic presumes to protest in the name of the law, they know how to square it, so that it complaisantly looks the other way while they go on with illicit enterprises—with the business, for example (it is Sir William Bragg who vouches for it), of teaching "the wave theory of light on Monday, Wednesday, and Friday, and the quantum theory on Tuesday, Thursday, and Saturday." It need not surprise us, then, to learn that physicists make nothing, when it suits their convenience, of regarding nucleus and electron, not as substances, but only as radiations—thus, casually dissolving the substantial world into a congeries of repellent and attractive velocities which we are invited to believe in because they can be mathematically identified and made use of. Perhaps, as Professor Jeans suggests, the world we live in was designed by a mathematician. Why not, indeed, if it can be most easily understood in terms of mathematical formulas? We know that two apples plus two apples make four apples. We have always taken it for granted that the apples exist, but we can very well understand that even if no apples are anywhere found it still remains true that two plus two make four. The mathematician gets on just as well without the apples, better indeed, since the apples have other attributes besides number. When sufficiently hard pressed, therefore, the physicist solves his difficulties by turning mathematician. As mathematician he can calculate the velocities that are observed to occur, meantime assuring us that the velocities could readily be attributed to substantial electrons, provided substantial electrons with such velocities should ever turn up. There is really no occasion for despair: our world can be computed even if it doesn't exist.

Perhaps I have said enough to suggest that the essential quality of the modern climate of opinion is factual rather than rational. The atmosphere which sustains our thought is so saturated with the actual that we can easily do with a minimum of the theoretical. We necessarily look at our world from the point of view of history and from the point of view of science. Viewed historically, it appears to be something in the making, something which can at best be only tentatively understood since it is not yet finished. Viewed scientifically, it appears as something to be accepted, something to be manipulated and mastered, something to adjust ourselves to with the least possible stress. So long as we can make efficient use of things, we feel no irresistible need to understand them. No doubt it is for this reason chiefly that the modern mind can be so wonderfully at ease in a mysterious universe.

III

All this is by way of introduction. I have chosen to say something about the political and social thought of the eighteenth century, something about the *Philosophes*. If I could stand on high and pronounce judgment on them, estimate authoritatively the value of their philosophy, tell wherein it is true, wherein false—if I could only do all this it would be grand. But this, unfortunately, is not possible. Living in the twentieth century, I am limited by the preconceptions of my age. It was therefore inevitable that I should approach the subject from the historical point of view; and if I have been at great pains to contrast the climate of opinion of Dante's time with that of our own, it is merely in order to provide the historical setting in which the ideas of the *Philosophes* may be placed. Before the historian can do anything with Newton and Voltaire, he has to make it clear that they came, historically speaking, after Dante and Thomas Aquinas and before Einstein and H. G. Wells. I assume that it will be worth while to place them in this relation, to look at them in this pattern, because the modern mind has a predilection for looking at men and things in this way; it finds a high degree of mental satisfaction in doing it; and mental satisfaction is always worth while, for the simple reason that when the mind is satisfied with the pattern of the things it sees, it has what it calls an "explanation" of the things—it has found the "cause" of them. My object is, therefore, to furnish an explanation of eighteenth-century thought, from the historical point of view, by showing that it was related to something that came before and to something else that came after.

We are accustomed to think of the eighteenth century as essentially modern in its temper. Certainly, the *Philosophes* themselves made a great point of having renounced the superstition and hocus-pocus of medieval Christian thought, and we have usually been willing to take them at their word. Surely, we say, the eighteenth century was preëminently the age of reason, surely the *Philosophes* were a skeptical lot, atheists in effect if not by profession, addicted to science and the scientific method, always out to crush the infamous, valiant defenders of liberty, equality, fraternity, freedom of speech, and what you will. All very true. And yet I think the *Philosophes* were nearer the Middle Ages, less emancipated from the preconceptions of medieval Christian thought, than they quite realized or we have commonly supposed. If we have done them more (or is it less?) than justice in giving them a good modern character, the reason is that they speak a familiar language. We read Voltaire more readily than Dante, and follow an argument by Hume more easily than one by Thomas Aquinas. But I think our appreciation is of the surface more than of the fundamentals of their thought. We agree with them more readily when they are witty and cynical than when they are wholly serious. Their negations rather than their affirmations enable us to treat them as kindred spirits.

But, if we examine the foundations of their faith, we find that at every turn the *Philosophes* betray their debt to medieval thought without being aware of it. They denounced Christian philosophy, but rather too much, after the manner of those who are but half emancipated from the "superstitions" they scorn. They had put off the fear of God, but maintained a respectful attitude toward the Deity. They ridiculed the idea that the universe had been created in six days, but still believed it to be a beautifully articulated machine designed by the Supreme Being according to a rational plan as an abiding place for mankind. The Garden of Eden was for them a myth, no doubt, but they looked enviously back to the golden age of Roman virtue, or across the waters to the unspoiled innocence of an Arcadian civilization that flourished in Pennsylvania. They renounced the authority of church and Bible, but exhibited a naïve faith in the authority of nature and reason. They scorned metaphysics, but were proud to be called philosophers. They dismantled heaven, somewhat prematurely it seems, since they retained their faith in the immortality of the soul. They courageously discussed atheism, but not before the servants. They defended toleration valiantly, but could with difficulty tolerate priests. They denied that miracles ever happened, but believed in the perfectibility of the human race. We feel that these Philosophers were at once too credulous and too skeptical. They were the victims of common sense. In spite of their rationalism and their humane sympathies, in spite of their aversion to hocus-pocus and enthusiasm and dim perspectives, in spite of their eager skepticism, their engaging cynicism, their brave youthful blasphemies and talk of hanging the last king in the entrails of the last priest—in spite of all of it, there is more of Christian philosophy in the writings of the *Philosophes* than has yet been dreamt of in our histories.

In the following lectures I shall endeavor to elaborate this theme. I shall attempt to show that the underlying preconceptions of eighteenth-century thought were still, allowance made for certain important alterations in the bias, essentially the same as those of the thirteenth century. I shall attempt to show that the *Philosophes* demolished the Heavenly City of St. Augustine only to rebuild it with more up-to-date materials.

II

The Laws of Nature and of Nature's God

Qu'est-ce que la loi naturelle? C'est
l'ordre régulier et constant des faits, par
lequel Dieu régit l'univers. VOLNEY.

I

WHEN we think of the *Philosophes* we think first of
all, and quite rightly, of certain French names so
much written about that they are familiar to all the
world—Montesquieu and Voltaire and Rousseau,
Diderot and Helvétius and Baron d'Holbach, Turgot and Quesnay and Condorcet, to mention only
the best known. If we were interested in the Enlightenment as a prelude to the Revolution we also
might conveniently forget, as most writers do, that
France was not the only country blessed (or cursed,
if you like) with Philosophers; but since we are concerned less with the consequences than with the preconceptions of the Enlightenment we will do well to
note that it is not a peculiarly French but an international climate of opinion that is in question. Leibnitz and Lessing and Herder, the young Goethe even
(in some of his varying moods); Locke and Hume
and Bolingbroke, Ferguson and Adam Smith, Price
and Priestley; and in the new world Jefferson, whose

33

sensitized mind picked up and transmitted every novel vibration in the intellectual air, and Franklin of Philadelphia, printer and friend of the human race—these also, whatever national or individual characteristics they may have exhibited, were true children of the Enlightenment. The philosophical empire was an international domain of which France was but the mother country and Paris the capital. Go where you like—England, Holland, Italy, Spain, America—everywhere you meet them, Philosophers speaking the same language, sustained by the same climate of opinion. They are of all countries and of none, having openly declared their allegiance to mankind, desiring nothing so much as to be counted "among the small number of those who by their intelligence and their works have merited well of humanity."[1] They are citizens of the world, the emancipated ones, looking out upon a universe seemingly brand new because so freshly flooded with light, a universe in which everything worth attending to is visible, and everything visible is seen to be unblurred and wonderfully simple after all, and evidently intelligible to the human mind—the mind of Philosophers.

There is one not unimportant point about the Philosophers that ought, in simple fairness to them, to be noted in passing, especially since few writers take the trouble to mention it: the Philosophers were not

[1] Grimm, *Correspondance littéraire*, IV, 69.

philosophers. I mean to say they were not professors of philosophy whose business it was to publish, every so often, systematic and stillborn treatises on epistemology and the like subjects. Exceptions there were no doubt. Leibnitz and Locke and Hume, Adam Smith perhaps, and maybe Helvétius will be found catalogued under philosophy and mentioned in formal histories of that subject. But for the most part the Philosophers were men of letters, writers of books intended to be read and designed to spread abroad new ideas or to shed new light on old ones. I need only mention that Voltaire wrote plays, histories, tales, and an *A B C* of Newtonian physics for ladies and gentlemen unblessed with a knowledge of mathematics; that Franklin was a scientist, inventor, politician, diplomat, political economist, moralist, and the first and most successful of American "columnists"; that Diderot, besides being the literary editor and promoter of the *Encyclopédie,* was a journalist who wrote on everything that struck his lively fancy—on art salons, the social implications of a mechanistic theory of the universe, the baneful effect of emotional repression on nuns; that Rousseau, in defense of the thesis that art is injurious to mankind, employed a high degree of art in the writing of political propaganda and didactic romances; that Mably wrote a long history to prove that France once possessed, but had somehow mislaid, a most admirable political constitution.

35

But if the Philosophers were not philosophers they had, like their modern counterparts, a philosophical message to deliver: they were the eager bearers of good tidings to mankind. Disinterested? Objectively detached? By no means. Do not look for these high virtues in the Philosophers, least of all when they make a point of them. No doubt the objective attitude may sometimes be found—in the scientific expositions of Newton and his confrères, in some of the writings of Franklin perhaps, or those of Hume. But to be amused and detached observers of the human scene was not characteristic of them. It is true you will find plenty of cynical wit—in Voltaire above all, as everyone knows. But the wit is too superficially cynical to be more than a counterirritant. There is more fundamental pessimism to be found in the seventeenth than in the eighteenth century, in the *Libertins* than in the *Philosophes*. The disillusionment of Hume and Franklin was deep enough, but it found easy release in a genial irony that disturbed no one, least of all themselves. The cynicism of Voltaire was not bred in the bone as the great Frederick's was; nor was it, like that of La Rochefoucauld, the cold-blooded systematization of a grand seignior's indifference; still less, like that of Pascal, a fatal spiritual malady troubling the heart. It was all on the surface, signifying nothing but the play of a supple and irrepressible mind, or the sharp impatience of an exasperated idealist. In spite of *Candide* and all the

36

rest of it, Voltaire was an optimist, although not a naïve one. He was the defender of causes, and not of lost causes either—a crusader pledged to recover the holy places of the true faith, the religion of humanity. Voltaire, skeptic—strange misconception! On the contrary, a man of faith, an apostle who fought the good fight, tireless to the end, writing seventy volumes to convey the truth that was to make us free.

At this point I ought perhaps to mention the well-worn word "enthusiasm." Do not the writers of the eighteenth century, the early eighteenth century, commonly insist on the just measure, the virtue of keeping cool and not straying beyond the call of common sense? Do they not even become a little heated and scornful when confronted with examples of "enthusiasm"? They do indeed, and there's the rub. To be scornful is not to be detached. The aversion of the Philosophers to enthusiasm did not carry them to the high ground of indifference. Their aversion to enthusiasm was itself an enthusiasm, a mark of their resolute rejection of all that was not evident to the senses, of their commendable passion for opening up and disinfecting all the musty, shuttered closets of the mind. The best case in point, the best and most ironical, is Hume, no less: Hume, the personification of common sense, stiffly priding himself on a Jove-like avoidance of enthusiasm. Who, indeed, was so well suited to be an indifferent observer of the human scene? He had the temperament for it, and his philosophical speculations left him quite without illusion, or should have, since they led him to the conclusion that the ultimate cause of things "has no more regard to good above ill than to heat above cold."[2] But a conclusion which left so little scope for enthusiasm was too much even for Hume. He writes in 1737:

I am at present castrating my work . . .; that is, endeavouring it shall give as little offence as possible. . . . This is a piece of cowardice. . . . But I was resolved not to be an enthusiast in philosophy, while blaming other enthusiasms.[3]

It seems oversubtle—avoiding enthusiasm to the point of refusing to press a pessimistic argument to its logical conclusion. I think Hume's real reason for soft-pedaling skepticism was the feeling that such negative conclusions were useless. He writes:

A man has but a bad grace who delivers a theory, however true, which . . . leads to a practice dangerous and pernicious. Why rake into those corners of nature, which spread a nuisance all around? . . . Truths which are *pernicious* to society, if any such there be, will yield to errors, which are salutary and *advantageous*.[4]

At all events, in mid career Hume abandoned philo-

[2] *Dialogues Concerning Natural Religion* (1907), p. 160.
[3] J. H. Burton, *Life and Correspondence of David Hume*, I, 64.
[4] *Essays* (1767), II, 352, 353.

sophical speculations for other subjects, such as history and ethics, which could be treated honestly without giving "offense," and from which useful lessons might be drawn. By this devious route the prince of skeptics, who abhorred enthusiasm with a pure passion, found his way into the company of those who might be regarded as having "deserved well of humanity."

In all this Hume is representative of his century. Its characteristic note is not a disillusioned indifference, but the eager didactic impulse to set things right. *Bienfaisance, humanité*—the very words, we are told, are new, coined by the Philosophers to express in secular terms the Christian ideal of service. In this connection one is reminded of that earnest and amiable and rather futile Abbé de Saint-Pierre, the man "at whom every one laughs, and who is alone serious and without laughter."[5] How industriously this priest labored in the secular vineyard of the Lord! How many "projects" he wrote, helpful hints for the improvement of mankind—"Project for Making Roads Passable in Winter," "Project for the Reform of Begging," "Project for Making Dukes and Peers Useful." And then one day, quite suddenly, so he tells us, "there came into my mind a project which by its great beauty struck me with astonishment. It has occupied all my attention for fif-

[5] Quoted from La Bruyère by Sainte-Beuve, *Lundis*, XV, 257.

teen days."[6] The result we know: *A Project for Making Peace Perpetual in Europe!*

Well, let us join the others and laugh at the Abbé, but does not his *penchant* for projects remind us of Jefferson, does not his passion for improvement recall Poor Richard? Let us laugh at him, by all means, but be well assured that when we do we are laughing at the eighteenth century, at its preoccupation with human welfare, at its *penchant* for projects. Who, indeed, was not, in this bright springtime of the modern world, making or dreaming of projects? What were most of the scientific academies in France doing but discussing, quarreling about, and having a jolly time over the framing of projects? What was the *Encyclopédie*, what was the Revolution itself? Grand projects, surely. What, indeed (the question stares us in the face), was this enlightened eighteenth century doing, what significance had it in the world anyway if not just this: that with earnest purpose, with endless argument and impassioned propaganda and a few not unhappy tears shed in anticipation of posterity's gratitude, it devoted all its energies to sketching the most naïvely simple project ever seen for making dukes and peers useful, for opening all roads available to the pursuit of happiness, for securing the blessings of liberty, equality, and fraternity to all mankind? Maybe this project

[6] Drouet, *Abbé de Saint-Pierre*, p. 108.

was less futile than those of the Abbé de Saint-Pierre, maybe it only seems so; but it was at all events inspired by the same ideal—the Christian ideal of service, the humanitarian impulse to set things right.

I do not forget that during the course of the century there is to be noted a change in the outward expression of this didactic impulse to set things right. Sometime about 1750, men of sense became men of sentiment, and presently men of sentiment began to weep. The tears of the later century have often been attributed to the influence of Rousseau, wrongly I think. It is certain that Diderot shed tears before he knew Rousseau, and continued to do so after he quarreled with him. As early as 1760, the practice was so common that the little Abbé Galiani shocked Diderot one day by confessing that *he* had never shed a tear in his life; and some years before the statement of Fontenelle that he had "relegated sentiment to the *églogue*" aroused in the cold and upright Grimm a feeling very near aversion.[7] Too much may easily be made of this change in manners. The reserve of a Fontenelle or the expansiveness of a Diderot were but outward characteristics—the outward evidence of an inward grace; an inward grace, they would have you know, far more efficacious than that of the religious. But the Philosophers were more akin

[7] *Correspondance littéraire*, III, 345.

to the religious than they knew. They were the secular bearers of the Protestant and the Jansenist tradition. Their aversion to enthusiasm was in truth but the measure of their irritation. It irritated them, the enlightened ones, to think that mankind had been so long deluded by priests and medicine men who had played their game, and still played it, by keeping the minds of the vulgar loosely wrapped in a warm, emotional fog. "It has taken centuries," exclaimed Grimm, "to subdue the human race to the tyrannical yoke of the priests; it will take centuries and a series of efforts and successes to secure its freedom."[8] We need not be deceived. In spite of their persiflage and wit, in spite of their correct manner and restrained prose, we can still hear, in the very accents of the saints, the despairing cry, "How long, O Lord, how long!"

Not so long, at that, if the Philosophers could have their way. And they were bent on having it. They were out for the cold facts, out to spoil the game of the mystery-mongers. That species of enthusiasm was indeed to be banned; but only to be replaced by an enthusiasm, however well concealed beneath an outward calm, for the simple truth of things. Knowing beforehand that the truth would make them free, they were on the lookout for a special brand of truth, a truth that would be on their side, a truth they could make use of in their business. Some sure

[8] *Correspondance littéraire*, V, 389.

instinct warned them that it would be dangerous to know too much, that "to comprehend all is to pardon all." They were too recently emancipated from errors to regard error with detachment, too eager to spread the light to enjoy the indolent luxury of the suspended judgment. Emancipated themselves, they were conscious of a mission to perform, a message to deliver to mankind; and to this messianic enterprise they brought an extraordinary amount of earnest conviction, of devotion, of enthusiasm. We can watch this enthusiasm, this passion for liberty and justice, for truth and humanity, rise and rise throughout the century until it becomes a delirium, until it culminates, in some symbolical sense, in that half admirable, half pathetic spectacle of June 8, 1794, when Citizen Robespierre, with a bouquet in one hand and a torch in the other, inaugurated the new religion of humanity by lighting the conflagration that was to purge the world of ignorance, vice, and folly.

Too much has been made of the negations of these crusaders of the age of reason: too much by the nineteenth century because it had no liking for the enlightened ones; too much by our own century because we have no liking for the Victorians. Their negations more often than not were mere surface cynicisms, and there is less in these surface cynicisms than we are apt to think. Take one of Voltaire's swift shining shafts of wit: "History is after all only a pack of tricks we play on the dead." Ah,

yes, how true it is, we say; and we are astonished
that Voltaire could have been so profound. Then we
realize that he did not really mean it. To him it was
a witticism intended to brand dishonest historians,
whereas we perceive that it formulated, in the neat-
est possible way, a profound truth—the truth that
all historical writing, even the most honest, is unconsciously subjective, since every age is bound, in spite
of itself, to make the dead perform whatever tricks it
finds necessary for its own peace of mind. And this
leads us to reconsider another of his sayings: "Nothing is more annoying than to be obscurely hanged."
And we wonder whether he understood all the implications of this pregnant saying as well as we do;
whether he understood as well as we do, or think we
do, that he and his brother *Philosophes* must have
fed their enthusiasm for liberty and justice not a little on the satisfaction they found in being conspicu-
ously hanged (if only in effigy) for their brave little
blasphemies.

But, if we have understood their negations too
well, we have accepted their affirmations, their pro-
fessions of faith, rather too much as a matter of
course. Let Voltaire define natural religion: "I understand by natural religion the principles of morality common to the human race."[9] If it does not
bore us too much we ask a perfunctory question,
What is morality? and pause not for an answer. If

[9] *Oeuvres* (1883–85), XXII, 419.

by chance we really attend to these affirmations they
puzzle us. Over against the Angelic Doctor's definition of natural law, set that of Volney:

> The regular and constant order of facts by which God
> rules the universe; the order which his wisdom presents
> to the sense and reason of men, to serve them as an
> equal and common rule of conduct, and to guide them,
> without distinction of race or sect, towards perfection and
> happiness.[10]

The language is familiar, but the idea, once we examine it critically, is as remote as that of Thomas
Aquinas. Important if true, we say; but how comes
it, we ask, that you are so well acquainted with God
and his purposes? Who told you, skeptic as we have
been led to suppose, that there is a regular and constant order of nature? And this animal man (that
"damned race" as the great Frederick defined it),
how can you be so sure that he knows what perfection is, or would be happy if he had it?

Indeed, it is all too simple, this dogmatic affirma-
tion. It assumes everything that most needs to be
proved, and begs every question we could think of
asking. These skeptics who eagerly assent to so much
strike our sophisticated minds as overcredulous. We
feel that they are too easily persuaded, that they are
naïve souls after all, duped by their humane sympathies, on every occasion hastening to the gate to

[10] *Oeuvres* (2d ed.), I, 249.

meet and welcome platitudes and thin panaceas. And so our jaded and somewhat morbid modern curiosity is at last aroused. We wish to know the reason for all this fragile optimism. We wish to know what it is that sustains this childlike faith, what unexamined prepossessions enable the Philosophers to see the tangled wilderness of the world in this symmetrical, this obvious and uncomplicated pattern. Have they perhaps had some recent revelation authorizing them to speak in the very accents of the voice of God? Across the decades we hear the timid vagabond from Geneva, in passion-laden tones, thunder his arrogant challenge in the teeth of an archbishop: "Is it simple, is it natural that God should go in search of Moses to speak to Jean Jacques Rousseau?"[11] Well, frankly, we do not know. But it seems obvious that Rousseau has up his sleeve some good answer to his own question, some answer that all the *Philosophes* will surely regard as conclusive. There must be, we begin to be aware, some private passageway to the heavenly throne, some secret backstairs entry that all the *Philosophes* know of, some door, closed to us, that will open to them when they give it a certain understood succession of raps. We should like to enter this door. We should really like to discover what it is that Jean Jacques Rousseau goes in search of when he wishes to know what God has said to him.

[11] *Oeuvres* (1823), VI, 115.

II

If we would discover the little backstairs door that for any age serves as the secret entranceway to knowledge, we will do well to look for certain unobtrusive words with uncertain meanings that are permitted to slip off the tongue or the pen without fear and without research; words which, having from constant repetition lost their metaphorical significance, are unconsciously mistaken for objective realities. In the thirteenth century the key words would no doubt be God, sin, grace, salvation, heaven, and the like; in the nineteenth century, matter, fact, matter-of-fact, evolution, progress; in the twentieth century, relativity, process, adjustment, function, complex. In the eighteenth century the words without which no enlightened person could reach a restful conclusion were nature, natural law, first cause, reason, sentiment, humanity, perfectibility (these last three being necessary only for the more tender-minded, perhaps).

In each age these magic words have their entrances and their exits. And how unobtrusively they come in and go out! We should scarcely be aware either of their approach or their departure, except for a slight feeling of discomfort, a shy self-consciousness in the use of them. The word "progress" has long been in good standing, but just now we are beginning to feel, in introducing it into the highest circles, the need of easing it in with quotation marks, that conventional apology that will save all our faces. Words of more ancient lineage trouble us more. Did not President Wilson, during the war, embarrass us not a little by appearing in public on such familiar terms with "humanity," by the frank avowal of his love for "mankind"? As for God, sin, grace, salvation—the introduction of these ghosts from the dead past we regard as inexcusable, so completely do their unfamiliar presences put us out of countenance, so effectively do they, even under the most favorable circumstances, cramp our style.

In the eighteenth century these grand magisterial words, although still to be seen, were already going out of fashion, at least in high intellectual society. It is true that theologians still made much of them, but even they felt called upon to offer a rational apology for doing so. Bishop Butler's famous *Analogy of Religion, Natural and Revealed* (1737) was only one, although one of the most elaborate and painstaking, of many exercises of this kind. But for the sophisticated, men of letters and men of the world, these masterful words were regarded with distaste. Unable to pronounce them without discomfort, enlightened "men of parts" commonly employed substitutes or euphemisms with less explicit, less compromising implications. The picture of salvation in the Heavenly City they toned down to a vague impressionistic image of a "future state," "immortality of the soul," or a more generalized earthly and social *félicité* or *perfectibilité du genre humain.* Grace was translated into virtue, virtue with a certain classical implication in the meaning—*ce fonds de rectitude et de bonté morale, qui est la base de la vertu,* as Marmontel defined it.[12] To be esteemed a "man of virtue" was both sufficient and efficacious, and likely to give one, without any painful searchings of the heart, the assurance of being in a state of social justification, or even, if the esteem were general enough, of complete sanctification. I suppose that Hume and Franklin, when they were in France, for example, must have had this assurance as fully as any saint of the church ever did.

With the Heavenly City thus shifted to earthly foundations, and the business of justification transferred from divine to human hands, it was inevitable that God should be differently conceived and more indifferently felt. Not that he could be (except by a few unnaturally hardened souls) dispensed with altogether. Most eighteenth-century minds were too accustomed to a stable society with fixed ranks, too habituated to an orderly code of manners and a highly conventionalized art, to be at all happy in a disordered universe. It seemed safer, therefore, even for the enlightened ones, to retain God, or some plausible substitute, as a kind of dialectical guaranty that all was well in the most comfortable of common-

[12] *Mémoires* (1818), II, 195.

sense worlds. But, obviously, the Creator as a mere first premise no longer needed those rich and all too human qualities of God the Father. Having performed his essential function of creation, it was proper for him to withdraw from the affairs of men into the shadowy places where absolute being dwells. Thus withdrawn, he ceased to be personal and inconvenient. No longer demanding propitiatory sacrifices, he could be regarded merely as that Omniscience or Beneficence which men of sense could serenely contemplate with respect untempered with fear or adoration. Yet, even men of sense needed some word for this necessary thing, some suitable substitute for God the Father. Supreme Being? Author of the Universe? Great Contriver? Prime Mover? First Cause? Surely, any of these would serve. We know at least, to our great discomfort, that all of them were freely used.

It would have been impossible, would it not, for the *Philosophes* to have thus complacently permitted God the Father to fade away into the thin abstraction of a First Cause unless they were prepared to dispense with his revelation to men—the revelation through Holy Writ and Holy Church. This was, indeed, the whole point of their high, offensive gesture. Renunciation of the traditional revelation was the very condition of being truly enlightened; for to be truly enlightened was to see the light in all its fulness, and the light in its fulness revealed two very simple and obvious facts. One of these contained the sum of those negations which we understand so well —the fact that the supposed revelation of God's purposes through Holy Writ and Holy Church was a fraud, or at best an illusion born of ignorance, perpetrated, or at least maintained, by the priests in order to accentuate the fears of mankind, and so hold it in subjection. The other fact contained the sum of those affirmations which we understand less easily—that God had revealed his purpose to men in a far more simple and natural, a far less mysterious and recondite way, through his works. To be enlightened was to understand this double truth, that it was not in Holy Writ, but in the great book of nature, open for all mankind to read, that the laws of God had been recorded. This is the new revelation, and thus at last we enter the secret door to knowledge. This open book of nature was what Jean Jacques Rousseau and his philosophical colleagues went in search of when they wished to know what God had said to them.

Nature and natural law—what magic these words held for the philosophical century! Enter that country by any door you like, you are at once aware of its pervasive power. I have but just quoted, in another connection, extracts from the writings of Hume, Voltaire, Rousseau, Volney: in each of them nature takes without question the position customarily reserved for the guest of honor. To find a proper title for this lecture I had only to think of the Declaration of Independence—"to assume, among the powers of the earth, the separate and equal station, to which the laws of nature and of nature's God entitle them." Turn to the French counterpart of the Declaration, and you will find that "the aim of every political association is the preservation of the natural and imprescriptible rights of man." Search the writings of the new economists and you will find them demanding the abolition of artificial restrictions on trade and industry in order that men may be free to follow the natural law of self-interest. Look into the wilderness of forgotten books and pamphlets dealing with religion and morality: interminable arguments, clashing opinions, different and seemingly irreconcilable conclusion you will find, and yet strangely enough controversialists of every party unite in calling upon nature as the sovereign arbiter of all their quarrels. The Christian Bishop Butler affirms with confidence that "the whole analogy of nature . . . most fully shews that there is nothing incredible in the general [Christian] doctrine of religion, that God will reward and punish men for their actions hereafter."[13] The deist Voltaire, rejecting the Christian doctrine of religion, asserts with equal dogmatism that "natural law . . . which nature teaches all men" is that "upon which all religion is founded."[14] The atheist Holbach, rejecting all religion, neverthe-

[13] *The Analogy of Religion, Natural and Revealed, to the Constitution and Course of Nature* (1900), p. 39.
[14] *Oeuvres,* XXV, 39; IX, 443.

less holds that "the morality suitable to man should be founded on the nature of man."[15] Christian, deist, atheist—all acknowledge the authority of the book of nature; if they differ it is only as to the scope of its authority, as to whether it merely confirms or entirely supplants the authority of the old revelation. In the eighteenth-century climate of opinion, whatever question you seek to answer, nature is the test, the standard: the ideas, the customs, the institutions of men, if ever they are to attain perfection, must obviously be in accord with those laws which "nature reveals at all times, to all men."[16]

Not that the concepts of nature and natural law were new in the world. Aristotle justified slavery on the ground that it was in accord with nature.[17] The stoic emperor, Marcus Aurelius, understood that "nothing is evil which is according to Nature."[18] Roman jurists endeavored to reconcile positive law with the law of nature and right reason. Thomas Aquinas knew that the "participation of the eternal law in the rational creature is called the natural law."[19] According to Calvin, "Natural equity . . . demands that princes be armed . . . to defend the subjects committed to their care whenever they are hostilely assailed."[20] Robert Barclay, the Quaker, tells us that

[15] *Système social,* I, 58.   [16] Voltaire, *Oeuvres,* XXV, 560.
[17] *Politics,* chaps. v, vi.   [18] *Meditations,* Bk. II, 17.
[19] *Summa theologica,* Part II (First Part), Q. XCI, art. ii.
[20] *Institutes,* Bk. IV, chap. xx, sec. 11.

"this forcing of men's consciences is contrary . . . to the very *law of nature*."[21] Vittoria, a Dominican professor, defined the law of nations as "that which natural reason establishes between all nations."[22] Suarez, the Jesuit philosopher, thought that the "natural light of intelligence, spontaneously pronouncing on that which should be done, may be called the natural law."[23] Grotius founded civil and international society on human nature, which is the "mother of . . . natural law."[24] English Levelers in the seventeenth century founded their revolt on the "laws of God and nature." Hobbes defended, and Locke refuted, the doctrine of despotic power on the same high ground. Montaigne, who welcomed and relished every idea that ever was, felt it not reasonable that "art should gain the pre-eminence of our great and powerful mother nature."[25] And, finally, not to try your patience further, Pascal was familiar enough with nature and all her ways to pronounce a final judgment. "But what is nature? Why is custom not natural? I much fear that this nature is itself only a first custom, as custom is second nature."[26]

Not the exclusive possession of the eighteenth century, this "ideal image" of nature; no, but after all a different, a more substantial image arises to charm

[21] *Apology*, XIV, sec. 4.
[22] Quoted in C. L. Lange, *Histoire de l'internationalisme*, I, 272.
[23] *Ibid.*, p. 281.
[24] *Rights of War and Peace*, Prolegomena, p. 16.
[25] *Essays*, Bk. I, chap. xxx.   [26] *Pensées* (1897), I, 42.

that century. In earlier centuries the ideal image of nature was, as one may say, too ghostly ever to be mistaken for nature herself. Nature herself had hitherto seemed to common sense intractable, even mysterious and dangerous, at best inharmonious to man. Men therefore desired some authoritative assurance that there was no need to be apprehensive; and this assurance came from theologians and philosophers who argued that, since God is goodness and reason, his creation must somehow be, even if not evidently so to finite minds, good and reasonable. Design in nature was thus derived *a priori* from the character which the Creator was assumed to have; and natural law, so far from being associated with the observed behavior of physical phenomena, was no more than a conceptual universe above and outside the real one, a logical construction dwelling in the mind of God and dimly reflected in the minds of philosophers.

Once safely within the eighteenth century we cease to be haunted by this ghostly ideal image. The ideal image is still with us, but it has taken on a more familiar and substantial body. No one ever looked more attentively at the eighteenth-century image of nature than Hume, who knew better than anyone else that it was an illusion; and for that very reason there is no better description of it than that which he put into the mouth of Cleanthes, one of the characters in his *Dialogues Concerning Natural Religion*. In defense of natural religion, Cleanthes says:

55

Look around the world: contemplate the whole and every part of it: You will find it to be nothing but one great machine, subdivided into an infinite number of lesser machines, which again admit of subdivisions, to a degree beyond what human senses and faculties can trace and explain. All these various machines, and even their most minute parts, are adjusted to each other with an accuracy, which ravishes into admiration all men, who have ever contemplated them. The curious adapting of means to ends, throughout all nature, resembles exactly, though it much exceeds, the productions of human . . . intelligence. Since therefore the effects resemble each other, we are led to infer . . . that the causes also resemble; and that the Author of Nature is somewhat similar to the mind of man; though possessed of much larger faculties, proportioned to the grandeur of the work, which he has executed.[27]

The passage is significant in two respects. We note at once that the logical process has been reversed. Cleanthes does not conclude that nature *must* be rational because God *is* eternal reason; he concludes that God *must* be an engineer because nature *is* a machine. From this reversal of the logical process it follows that natural law is identified with the actual behavior of nature. What ravishes Cleanthes into admiration is not the exceeding beauty of a logical concept of the world, but the exceeding intricacy and delicate adjustment of the world itself. For him nature is not a logical concept, but a sub-

[27] *Dialogues* (1907), p. 30.

stantial reality; and natural law, instead of being a construction of deductive logic, is the observed harmonious behavior of material objects.

This transformation of the ideal image of nature was the result, as everyone knows, of the scientific discoveries of the seventeenth century. Galileo observed that the pendulum behaved in a certain manner, and then formulated the law of the pendulum in terms of mathematics. Newton did not doubt that the heavens declare the glory of God; but he was concerned to find out, by looking through a telescope and doing a sum in mathematics, precisely how they managed it. He discovered that every particle of matter, whether in the heavens or elsewhere, behaved as if it attracted every other particle with a force proportional to the product of the masses and inversely proportional to the square of the distance. This was a new kind of "law of nature." Formerly, as the editor of the second edition of the *Principia* tells us, philosophers were "employed in giving names to things, and not in searching into things themselves." Newton himself noted the difference by saying: "These Principles I consider not as occult Qualities, supposed to result from the specific Forms of Things, but as general Laws of Nature, by which the Things themselves are form'd."[28] This was the new way to knowledge opened up by "natural

[28] Quoted in Dampier-Whetham, *A History of Science*, pp. 181, 183.

philosophy": to "search into Things themselves," and then to formulate the "general Laws of Nature by which the Things themselves are form'd."

Certainly, this new philosophy ravished the eighteenth century into admiration; and not the least astonishing thing about it was the commonplace methods employed to discover such marvelous truths. That Newton discovered the nature of light seemed even less significant to his contemporaries than that he did so by playing with a prism. It was as if nature had for the first time been brought close to men, close enough to be tangible and clearly visible in all its wonderful details. Nature, it seemed, was, after all, just the common things that common men observed and handled every day, and natural law only the uniform way these things behaved. Steam bubbling from the spout of a kettle, smoke whisking up a chimney, morning mist lifting from meadows—here was nature all about, moving in ways not mysterious her wonders to perform; and revealing, to the eyes of common men, no less than to the learned, those laws that imposed on all things their reasonable and beneficent, even if curious and intricate, commands.

When philosophy became a matter of handling test tubes instead of dialectics everyone could be, in the measure of his intelligence and interest, a philosopher. As Goethe tells us:

Many a one became convinced that nature had endowed him with as great a portion of good and straight-forward sense as, perchance, he required to form such a clear notion of objects that he could manage them and turn them to his own profit, and that of others, without laboriously troubling himself about the most universal problems. . . . Men made the trial, opened their eyes, looked straight before them, observant, industrious, active. . . .

. . . every one was now entitled, not only to philoso-phize, but also by degrees to consider himself a philoso-pher. Philosophy, therefore, was more or less sound and practised common sense, which ventured to enter upon the universal, and to decide upon inner and outer experi-ences. . . . and thus at last philosophers were found in all the faculties, nay, in all classes and trades.[29]

"Until philosophers become kings, . . . cities will not cease from ill," said Plato; but philosophy is perhaps in an even better way to exert influence (whether for good or ill) when common men become philosophers. The reason is that common men take up philosophy, if at all, not as an exercise in dialec-tic, but as something that holds for them the assur-ance of a better way of life. They are apt, therefore, to associate any philosophy that interests them with the name of some great man, whom they can love or hate for having given the world a new idea; and they are sure to invest the new idea with some meaning

[29] *Autobiography* (Bohn ed.), I, 231; *Sämmtliche Werke*, XXIII, 71.

that it did not originally have. We are familiar with this procedure, having noted, during the last fifty years, the association of the "evolutionary philosophy" with the name of Darwin, and the transformation of "Darwinism" into "monkeyism" or the "white man's burden" as the case may be—into something at all events which Darwin, simple man, would be astonished to hear of. The same thing happened in the eighteenth century. Common men associated the new philosophy with the name of Newton because it appeared that Newton, more than any other man, had banished mystery from the world by discovering a "universal law of nature," thus demonstrating, what others had only asserted, that the universe was rational and intelligible through and through, and capable, therefore, of being subdued to the uses of men.

The "Newtonian philosophy" was, accordingly, as familiar to common men in the middle eighteenth century as the "Darwinian philosophy" is in our day. "Very few people read Newton," Voltaire explained, "because it is necessary to be learned to understand him. But *everybody talks about him.*"[30] Why, indeed, should ordinary men read Newton? They were not greatly interested in the proposition that "reaction is always equal and opposite to action." They were interested in the Newtonian philosophy, a very different thing. No need to open the

[30] *Oeuvres*, XXII, 130.

Principia to find out what the Newtonian philosophy was—much better not, in fact. Leave that to the popularizers, who could find in the *Principia* more philosophy than common men could, very often more, I must say, than Newton himself ever did. Anyone might open, instead of the *Principia*, Benjamin Martin's *A Plain and Familiar Introduction to the Newtonian Philosophy, in Six Sections, Illustrated by Six Copper-Plates* (1751), of which there appeared in due time five editions; or James Ferguson's *Astronomy Explained upon Sir Isaac Newton's Principles, and Made Easy to Those who have not Studied Mathematics* (1756), which ran to seven editions; or Voltaire's *Éléments de la philosophie de Newton*, which could be read in English (1738) as well as in the original French; or Count Algorotti's *Il Newtonianismo per le dame*, which ran to three editions in Italian, was translated into French (1738), and into English under the title *Theory of Light and Colors* (1739); or (for those poetically inclined) J. T. Desaguliers' *The Newtonian System of the World the Best Model of Government, an Allegorical Poem* (1728).

In these books, or in others like them, common men could find the Newtonian philosophy, a philosophy which was of interest to them, not so much for the scientific discoveries it set forth as for the bearing of those discoveries upon the most fundamental of human problems—that is to say, the relation of man to nature and of both to God. What those relations were, or were taken to be, is admirably stated by Colin Maclaurin, Professor of Mathematics in the University of Edinburgh, in his book, *An Account of Sir Isaac Newton's Philosophical Discoveries,* perhaps the ablest of the popular expositions in English.

To describe the *phenomena* of nature, to explain their causes . . . and to inquire into the whole constitution of the universe, is the business of natural philosophy. A strong curiosity has prompted men in all times to study nature; every useful art has some connexion with this science; and the inexhausted beauty and variety of things makes it ever agreeable, new, and surprising.

But natural philosophy is subservient to purposes of a higher kind, and is chiefly to be valued as it lays a sure foundation for natural religion and moral philosophy; by leading us, in a satisfactory manner, to the knowledge of the Author and Governor of the universe. . . .

We are, from his works, to seek to know God, and not to pretend to mark out the scheme of his conduct, in nature, from the very deficient ideas we are able to form of that great mysterious Being. . . .

Our views of Nature, however imperfect, serve to represent to us, in the most sensible manner, that mighty power which prevails throughout, acting with a force and efficacy that appears to suffer no diminution from the greatest distances of space or intervals of time; and that wisdom which we see equally displayed in the exquisite structure and just motions of the greatest and subtilest parts. These, with perfect goodness, by which they are evidently directed, constitute the supreme object of the speculations of a philosopher; who, while he contemplates and admires so excellent a system, cannot but be himself *excited and animated to correspond with the general harmony of nature.*[81]

The closing words of this passage may well be taken as a just expression of the prevailing state of mind about the middle of the eighteenth century. Obviously the disciples of the Newtonian philosophy had not ceased to worship. They had only given another form and a new name to the object of worship: having denatured God, they deified nature. They could, therefore, without self-consciousness, and with only a slight emendation in the sacred text, repeat the cry of the psalmist: "I will lift up mine eyes to Nature from whence cometh my help!" With eyes uplifted, contemplating and admiring so excellent a system, they were excited and animated to correspond with the general harmony.

III

The desire to correspond with the general harmony springs perennial in the human breast. Saints of all ages have aspired to become one with whatever gods there be. In medieval times the approved method, in Europe, was thought to be fasting and prayer, denial of the flesh, the renunciation of the

[81] *Newton's Philosophical Discoveries* (1775), pp. 3, 4, 95.

natural man. "Who shall deliver me from the body of this death!" The physical dwelling place of the spirit was thought to be a disharmony, a soiled and cloying vesture of decay closing in and blinding the spirit so that, during its earthly pilgrimage, it could only with difficulty, if at all, enter into the harmony that was God. But the enlightened ones knew that it was not so. From this darkness also they had emerged into the light which enabled them to see that the natural and the spiritual man were but different manifestations of one harmonious whole.

The rationalization of this will to believe was provided by John Locke in his epoch-making book, *An Essay Concerning Human Understanding,* which became the psychological gospel of the eighteenth century. Its great service to the men of that time was to demonstrate that the mind owed nothing to inheritance, to "innate ideas"; everything to environment, to the sensations that flowed in upon it from the outer world. A modern critic assures us that the theory of innate ideas which Locke demolished was "so crude that it is difficult to suppose that any serious thinker ever held it."[32] That may well be. Maybe serious thinkers are few, and maybe the world is ruled by crude ideas. What Locke aimed at no doubt, what the eighteenth century acclaimed him for having demolished, was the Christian doctrine of total

[32] C. C. J. Webb, *Studies in the History of Natural Theology,* p. 354.

depravity, a black, spreading cloud which for centuries had depressed the human spirit. For if, as Locke maintained, the mind at birth was devoid of implanted and ineradicable ideas and dispositions, was in fact no more than a blank white sheet of paper upon which the outer world of nature and human association was to write whatever of good or ill repute might be found recorded there, why, then, the mind of man was a record made by that outer world: jazzed and discordant now that the outer world was so; a satisfying and ordered symphony when that outer world should become, as it might, what men had conceived it ought to be. This was Locke's great title to glory, that he made it possible for the eighteenth century to believe with a clear conscience what it wanted to believe, namely, that since man and the mind of man were shaped by that nature which God had created, it was possible for men, "barely by the use of their natural faculties,"[33] to bring their ideas and their conduct, and hence the institutions by which they lived, into harmony with the universal natural order. With what simple faith the age of enlightenment welcomed this doctrine! With what sublime courage it embraced the offered opportunity to refashion the outward world of human institutions according to the laws of nature and of nature's God!

[33] *An Essay Concerning Human Understanding*, Bk. I, chap. ii, sec. 1.

I need not say that the difficulties were great: endless difficulties in the realm of practice; one fundamental difficulty in the realm of theory. Hidden away in the elaborate structure of Locke's *Essay* was a most disconcerting corollary. It was this: if nature be the work of God, and man the product of nature, then all that man does and thinks, all that he has ever done or thought, must be natural, too, and in accord with the laws of nature and of nature's God. Pascal had long since asked the fundamental question: "Why is custom not natural?" Why, indeed! But if all is natural, then how could man and his customs ever be *out of harmony* with nature? No doubt the difficulty could be avoided by declaring that there was no disharmony.

> All are but parts of one stupendous whole,
> Whose body nature is, and God the soul;
>
> . . . .
>
> All discord, harmony not understood;
> All partial evil, universal good:
> And, spite of pride, in erring reason's spite,
> One truth is clear, *Whatever is, is right.*

But this, addressed to the intelligence, was not an answer; it was merely an avoidance, a dishonest begging of the question. To assert that all that is, is right, was to beat all meaning out of the word "right," unless indeed one were willing to hood one's eyes once more in the cloak of Christian faith. For

66

Pope was merely repeating St. Thomas, who had written twenty volumes to reassure a world on the verge of doubt—twenty volumes to say that it was really right that things should be wrong, God only knows why.

A poet in search of peace and epigrams might be permitted to repeat the ancient theologians, but the Philosophers could not do so unless they were willing to renounce their premises or deny the evidence of common sense. The very foundation of the new philosophy was that the existence of God, if there was one, and his goodness, if goodness he could claim, must be inferred from the observable behavior of the world. Following Newton, the Philosophers had all insisted on this to the point of pedantry, and so, even, had the enlightened Christian theologians in their desperate effort to find arguments to convince doubting Thomases. How then could Philosophers say that all was somehow good in God's sight unless they could also say that there was no evil to be observed in the world of nature and man? Yet to say that there was no evil in the world—a world where Lisbon earthquakes occurred, where Bastilles functioned, where crowds still gathered to gloat over the lingering agony of men broken on the wheel—was an insult to common sense. No, whatever Locke may have done, he had done nothing to solve, even if for the unwary he had done much to obscure, the problem of evil in the world.

Before the middle of the century Hume had taken up this world-old problem, had looked at it straight, had examined it attentively round and round about; and then, in his *Dialogues Concerning Natural Religion,* with all the dialectical resources of the new philosophy, with a penetrating insight matched only by the serene urbanity with which he displayed it, had remorselessly exposed the futility of reason to establish either the existence or the goodness of God. "Epicurus's old questions are yet unanswered. Is he [God] willing to prevent evil, but not able? Then he is impotent. Is he able, but not willing? Then he is malevolent. Is he both able and willing? Whence then is evil?"[84] In the end Hume manages to chevy Christian mystics and atheists into the same camp, since they obviously agree on the main point, that reason is totally incompetent to answer ultimate questions; and so he concludes with that masterpiece of irony: "To be a philosophical Sceptic is, in a man of letters, the first and most essential step towards being a sound, believing Christian."[85] To read Hume's *Dialogues* after having read, with sympathetic understanding, the earnest deists and optimistic philosophers of the early century, is to experience a slight chill, a feeling of apprehension. It is as if, at high noon of the Enlightenment, at the hour of the siesta when everything seems so quiet and secure all about, one were suddenly aware of a short, sharp

[84] *Dialogues,* p. 134.　　　　[85] *Ibid.,* p. 191.

slipping of the foundations, a faint far-off tremor running underneath the solid ground of common sense.

There it was then—the ugly dilemma, emerging from the beautiful premises of the new philosophy: if nature is good, then there is no evil in the world; if there is evil in the world, then nature is so far not good. How will they meet it, the enlightened ones who with so much assurance and complacent wit have set out with the rule of reason to rebuild an unlovely universe according to nature's design? Will they, closing their eyes to the brute facts, maintain that there is no evil in the world? In that case there is nothing for them to set right. Or will they, keeping their eyes open, admit that there is evil in the world? In that case nature fails to provide them with any standard for setting things right. They have followed reason faithfully. Will they follow her to the end? She is pointing in two directions: back toward Christian faith; forward toward atheism. Which way will they choose? It does not really matter much, since in either case she will vanish at last, leaving them to face existence with no other support than hope, or indifference, or despair.

Well, we know what the Philosophers did in this emergency. They found, as we all find when sufficiently hard pressed, that reason is amenable to treatment. They therefore tempered reason with sentiment, reasons of the heart that reason knows not of; or held it in leash by experience, the universal judgment of mankind; or induced it to delay its pronouncements in view of the possibility (which in a pinch might be taken as a fact) that the world was after all neither a completed drama nor a perfected machine, but rather something as yet unfinished, something still in the making. It will be the purpose of the following lectures to elaborate these statements, to show how the Philosophers, still following reason, perhaps wisely, but certainly none too well, went on to finish and to furnish and to make resplendent the Heavenly City of their dreams.

III

The New History: Philosophy Teaching by Example

[L'histoire] nous fera voir, pour ainsi dire, l'homme en détail, après que la morale nous fait voir en gros. FONTENELLE.

[History's] chief use is only to discover the constant and universal principles of human nature. HUME.

I

BRUNETIERE somewhere mentions the fact that official documents, whatever their nature, are not drafted in order that history may be written from them. It does seem, I must say, that people living in past times often act as if the convenience of the future historian were a matter of negligible importance. If Hume had only published his *Dialogues Concerning Natural Religion* when it was written, he might have saved me much trouble. Had he published his book I might have shown that it was read by other Philosophers—Diderot and Holbach, for example; I might have found that Jefferson had a copy in his library, or that Franklin had mentioned, in a letter perhaps, having been impressed by this profound work: from all of which (and from much else of the same sort) I could no doubt have traced

71

the "influence," as it is called, of Hume's *Dialogues,* and happily concluded maybe that as a result of this influence philosophy, becoming aware of a logical dilemma in her path, turned away from rationalistic speculation to the study of history, morality, and politics. And the beginning of this new venture on philosophy's part I might conveniently have placed at the exact date when Hume's *Dialogues* was published. Unfortunately, owing to his indifference to my problem, all I can say is that Hume discreetly locked the manuscript away in his desk, so that it was quite unknown (except to a few intimate friends) until after his death.

A history lost and all for the want of a petty date! It is a tragedy not often met with, I admit. There are, nevertheless, compensations. With Hume's manuscript safely locked up in his desk, we shall at least not be taken in by the naïve notion that certain philosophers became atheists because they had read Hume's *Dialogues.* It has long been a favorite pastime of those who interest themselves in the history of culture to note the transfer of ideas (as if it were no more than a matter of borrowed coins) from one writer to another; to note, for example, that Mr. Jones must have got a certain idea from Mr. Smith because it can be shown that he had read, or might have read, Mr. Smith's book; all the while forgetting that if Mr. Jones hadn't already had the idea, or something like it, simmering in his own mind he wouldn't have cared to read Mr. Smith's book, or, having read it, would very likely have thrown it aside, or written a review to show what a bad and mistaken book it was. And how often it happens that books "influence" readers in ways not intended by the writers! We know that Madame Roland read the works of Holbach and Helvétius; but these works, instead of making her an atheist, only fortified her belief in God, so that she turned, more readily than she might otherwise have done, to Rousseau for consolation.

It is well to know that Hume locked his *Dialogues* away in his desk, but it is far more important to understand why he should have thought it worth while to write the work in the first place. Refusing to publish the manuscript made as little difference then as reprinting the book does now. Today anyone may read the *Dialogues,* but few people are sufficiently interested in the issues it raises to do so; in Hume's day no one could read the *Dialogues,* but the issues it raised were so important and so familiar that no one needed to. The issues raised were, for that century, fundamental. It was as if a rumor, started no one knew when, had at last become too insistent to be longer disregarded: the rumor that God, having departed secretly in the night, was about to cross the frontiers of the known world and leave mankind in the lurch. What we have to realize is that in those years God was on trial. The affair was nothing less than the intellectual *cause célèbre* of the age, and one which stirred the emotions of men in a way we can with difficulty understand. Not many men, not many Philosophers even, were likely to be troubled by the logical dilemma that interested Hume and Diderot and Berkeley; but everyone, the readers as well as the writers of books, was concerned to know whether there was a God to care for his immortal soul, or no God and no immortal soul to care for. It was in this guise that the dilemma, which I pictured at the close of the last lecture as emerging from the premises of the new philosophy, appeared to the common run of men: Were they living in a world ruled by a beneficent mind, or in a world ruled by an indifferent force? That was the question which, in this cynical age of reason, men could become heated over, a question debated everywhere—in books, in the pulpit, in the salons, at dinners over the wine, after the servants had retired—and we can no more think of a Philosopher ignorant of, or indifferent to, this question than we can think of a modern philosopher ignorant of, or indifferent to, the quantum theory. What concerns us is to know how the Philosophers met and disposed of this profound question.

Well, we know that there was in France, after the middle of the century, a little huddled company of rationalistic *enragés* who became famous, or infamous rather, by openly professing the creed of atheism—Holbach and Helvétius and La Mettrie and Meslier, to mention those who most counted. They did not lack courage, these *enragés*. They had the courage of their logic, and made it a point of pride or of bravado not to desert the Goddess of Reason after having been so well served by her. The Goddess had guided them safely out of the long night of superstition into the light of day, and for that they could not be too grateful. Were they then timorously to desert her because she showed them a world, filled with light, indeed, but unsubdued, uncharted, unlandscaped? No! They would follow Reason still (even if Reason turned out to be no goddess, but merely their own reasoning) into the wilderness of a world which to all appearance was neither good nor bad in itself, but good or bad only in so far as men might by their own unaided efforts make it, or fail to make it, serve their purposes.

Were they not read, these atheists? Did they not exert an "influence"? Yes, indeed. Everybody read them, or, better still, heard their doctrines whispered about. Everybody read them, but "almost everybody was terrified." They were beyond the pale, these atheists. Let us not forget their social isolation: the shocked feeling, in the outside world, of something obscene and blasphemous going on under cover of night at Holbach's house; the furtive sense of daring adventure into unconventional and abandoned circles with which many visitors (Philosophers some of

them) came away from those famed dinners. Let us
try to recover, if it be at all possible, the feeling of
grim desolation with which the young Goethe read,
and discussed with his fellow student, Holbach's
Système de la nature—that daring book, daring to
the point of denying the existence of God and the
immortality of the soul. "We could not conceive,"
Goethe tells us, "how such a book could be dangerous. It came to us so gray, so Cimmerian, so corpse-
like, that we could hardly endure its presence; we
shuddered before it, as if it had been a spectre."[1]

This was the influence of the "atheist" writings—
they made men shudder. Yet the atheists were only
following the Goddess of all the Philosophers (Rousseau perhaps excepted). Holbach's book, as Morley
says, pointed to

the finger of their own divinity, Reason, writing on the
wall the appalling judgments that there is no God; that
the universe is only matter in spontaneous motion; and,
most grievous word of all, that what men call their souls
die with the death of the body, as music dies when the
strings are broken.[2]

Appalling is perhaps not quite the word. Appalling
to the general run of readers, no doubt; but other
Philosophers had followed Reason as faithfully as
Holbach had, and were as familiar with her judg-

[1] Morley, *Diderot*, II, 175; *Sämmtliche Werke*, XXIV, 52.
[2] *Diderot*, II, 175.

ments. Nevertheless, when the Goddess pointed to her judgments the Philosophers, almost without exception, refused to accept them; instead of looking at the writing on the wall, they turned their backs and edged away, giving one excuse or other.

Each Philosopher might, of course, have his own special reason for deserting the Goddess. We know that Franklin, who as a boy stranded in London had published an atheistical work, later repented of that act of youthful braggadocio and dismissed the whole stupendous question by the casual remark that while a mechanical theory of the universe might be true it was "not very useful"; certainly not very useful to him, a respectable printer and politician living in Philadelphia, or famous as a defender of liberty at the Court of St. James's. We know that Hume had exhausted the dialectical approach to knowledge and that the truths he arrived at were, on his own confession, inadequately founded. Besides, the lonely man, tucked away in a provincial corner of the world, craved the applause of his fellows; and the disconcerting fact was that his speculative books not only did not sell, but were not well received by his friends. They lacked, as Hutchinson told him, "a certain warmth in the cause of virtue, which . . . all good men would relish."[3] Hume certainly took no pleasure in being regarded as the cold and finished

[3] J. H. Burton, *Life and Correspondence of David Hume,* I, 112, 113.

skeptic, a destroyer of illusions. He was much more ambitious "to be esteemed a man of virtue than a writer of taste"; and the fact that his history won for him the popularity he craved naturally confirmed him in the belief that it was useless to search into "those corners of nature that spread a nuisance all around." These are, no doubt, the reasons why Hume locked his *Dialogues* away in his desk, the reason why his contemporaries, could they have looked into that locked desk, would have found a most extraordinary, a most perplexing conclusion to the brilliant argument that demolished the foundations of natural religion; the conclusion, namely, that any "person seasoned with a just sense of the imperfections of natural reason, will fly to revealed truth with the greatest avidity."[4] Hume did not exactly fly to revealed truth; but he refused to publish his *Dialogues,* and never, in public at least, failed to exhibit a punctiliously correct attitude toward the Author of the Universe.

As for Voltaire—well, Voltaire, who had a horror of being duped, lets us know in many an aside that he is aware of the judgments on the wall to which the Goddess is pointing. What, no God? It may be. But if so, then it is necessary to invent one—for the people more especially, since they will never be sufficiently enlightened to understand that nature, blind as she may be, is good enough if she is good enough

[4] *Dialogues,* p. 191.

to bring forth a Voltaire now and then. As for the Philosophers, they will do well to let insoluble questions ride, and confine themselves to the cultivation of their gardens, being well assured that it will always be worth while to uproot the infamous things found growing therein.

Diderot, a far more interesting case than Voltaire, is often classed with the atheists. But the significant point for us is that this atheist, convinced against his will, is of another opinion still. Like Hume, he wrote speculative works (*La physiologie* and *L'entretien*) in which he reached the conclusion that the world is mechanically determined, that man is an accident, the soul is "nothing without the body," good will is nothing but "the last impulse of desire and aversion," and vice and virtue are mere words signifying nothing. Diderot the rationalist wrote these works. But there was another Diderot who refused to publish them; Diderot the man of virtue, whose warm heart told him with even greater assurance that vice and virtue were the most real of realities. This conflict between the two Diderots, between the fertile brain and the tempestuous heart, is revealed in *Le neveu de Rameau,* his one masterpiece, a dialogue as brilliant in its way as Hume's *Dialogues,* and concerned with the same dilemma. But unlike Hume's *Dialogues, Le neveu de Rameau* ends without any solution, not even a Pickwickian solution. Diderot had none of Hume's serenity, and to the end of his days his soul was filled with discord; his mind unable to find any sufficient reason for virtuous conduct, his heart unable to renounce the conviction that nothing is better in this world than to be a good man.[5]

From all of Diderot's writings there emerges an anxious concern for morality. He tells us that to have written some great constructive work on that subject was what he would "recall with the greatest satisfaction" in his last moments; but, he says,

I have not even dared to write the first line: I say to myself, if I do not come out of the attempt victorious, I become the apologist of wickedness; I will have betrayed the cause of virtue. . . . I do not feel myself equal to this sublime work; I have uselessly consecrated my whole life to it.[6]

In this concern for "morality," Diderot was typical of his generation; generally speaking, the Philosophers were all, like Hume and Diderot, ambitious to be esteemed "men of virtue." The reason is precisely that they were, from the point of view of their opponents, enemies of morality and virtue; and what, indeed, could justify all their negations, all their attacks on Christian faith and doctrine, if they were unable to replace the old morality by a new and

---

[5] For a fuller treatment of the dilemma of Diderot, see the *Philosophical Review*, XXIV, 54.

[6] *Oeuvres* (1875–77), II, 345.

more solidly based one? That unbelief would unsettle the foundations of morality and social order was the most effective charge which Christian apologists could possibly make against the Philosophers. "Philosophy" had to meet this charge. "It is not enough," said Diderot, referring to the theologians, "to know more than they do: it is necessary to show them that we are better, and that philosophy makes more good men than sufficient or efficacious grace."[7]

Well, it would be difficult, would it not, for philosophy to make more good men than sufficient or efficacious grace if it could offer nothing more reassuring than the doctrine that "the original source of things has no more regard to good above ill than to heat above cold." There is a profound significance in Diderot's feeling that it would be better not to defend virtue at all than to fail in the attempt; a philosopher who, having demolished the foundations of Christian morality, should fail to provide a natural foundation for it, would indeed be, in the eyes of common men, "an apologist for wickedness." Morality and social order had so long been founded on faith in God, the good life had so confidently been associated with an overruling Providence, that the prospect of a world in which men should be left to their own devices, unguarded against the evil impulses of the natural man, was not all at once to be contemplated with equanimity. Apart from all con-

[7] *Ibid.*, XIX, 464.

scious motives and personal considerations, the Philosophers instinctively felt that to profess atheism would be no less a confession of failure than to return like lost sheep to the Christian fold. Atheist! The very word, in that climate of opinion, sounded ominous, ribald, antisocial. Enlightened? Surely the Philosophers were enlightened. But the essence of enlightenment was intellectual security, the most prized possession of the Philosopher was assured knowledge; and what was atheism if not a confession of ignorance? Locked away in Hume's desk was the proof of it: the Christian mystic, Demea, and the skeptic, Philo, following Reason to the bitter end, found themselves in the same camp, agreeing only in this, that Reason is incompetent to answer any fundamental question about God, or morality, or the meaning of life. The Philosophers could not afford to accept this conclusion. For more than half a century they had leveled the batteries of Reason and common sense against the strongholds of ignorance and superstition: had made a great noise in the world in order that men might be more enlightened, society more solidly based, morality and virtue more secure. What a fiasco, then, would all this noise of battle have been for them had they been compelled in the end to put off their complaisant optimism, to renounce their dogmatism, to cease their clamor—to announce, in short, to an expectant world, in a small voice, this: "Reason tells us after all that there is no

God, that the universe is only matter in spontaneous motion, and that, like the priests whom we have denounced for their ignorance, we also, we Philosophers, know nothing."

I would not leave the impression that the Philosophers began to cold-shoulder abstract reason merely, or chiefly, because they found a logical dilemma in the path; still less that they embraced the cause of virtue with greater emotional warmth because they could find no ultimate reason for embracing it at all. There may be something in all that—I am inclined to think there is; but I do not wish to make too much of it. The Philosophers were certainly in need of a little intellectual collateral to guarantee their bright promises, to maintain their professional solvency; but quite apart from that they were, like other men, carried along by the strong social currents of the time. Hume's turning away from speculation to the study of history, economics, and politics was symptomatic of a certain change in the climate of opinion—of an increasing interest in the concrete political and social activities of men, and of the disposition to approach such matters in a more earnest temper, a mood more highly charged with emotion. Rousseau is the chief representative of this new mood, but he did not create it. To be convinced of this we need only look into the literary news sheet that was edited, during the years 1753–68, by Melchior Grimm. Let us look over the shoulder of the industrious and firm-lipped

Grimm as he runs through the new books just after
the middle of the century. Boileau, he reports in
1755, is little read because satire is no longer popular. And the fact recorded is not more significant
than Grimm's comment on it; satire, he thinks, calls
for the lowest order of talent, and since it is merely
destructive is essentially useless.[8] In the same year
he notes that Condillac's *Traité des sensations* was
not well received, which he attributes to the fact that
besides being too diffuse it is too cold, too lacking
in "philosophical imagination."[9] He complains that
politics is the most backward of sciences;[10] but notes
with satisfaction that otherwise the study of *useful*
subjects (agriculture, commerce, history, morality)
was never so general.[11] To study useful things, to approach them seriously, *en philosophe*, to impart to
them a certain imaginative warmth—how much better this was than to expose the feebleness of reason
and the uncertain foundations of knowledge!

The age of reason had scarcely run half its course
before the Philosophers were admitting the feebleness of reason, putting the ban on flippancy, and
turning to the study of useful, that is to say, factual,
subjects. In the succeeding decades the trend of interest toward the concrete and the practical, the
increasing preoccupation of thinking men with questions of political and social reform, and the rising

[8] *Correspondance littéraire*, II, 214. [9] *Ibid.*, III, 111.
[10] *Ibid.*, p. 97. [11] *Ibid.*, II, 170–171, 506.

temperature of the climate of opinion are every year
more apparent. The time had gone by when states-
men could afford to "let sleeping dogs lie"; when
kings could say with a straight face "I am the state."
In these years, when a tide in the affairs of men was
carrying them on to disaster, kings were under pressure to declare, with Frederick the Great, "I am the
first servant of the state." It was everywhere the
fashion, therefore, for rulers to turn benevolent in
order to mitigate the despotism that was denied
them, and to talk of reforms even if they made none;
while young princes, their successors to be, were
urged to engage, under the tutorial system established by the Philosophers, in the study of history in
order to learn, from the experience of mankind, what
was "requisite in a prince charged with the amelioration of society."[12]

The amelioration of society was the very thing
Philosophers had most at heart, and surely it was
eminently fitting that they should be called in to tutor princes in that benevolent art. It was unfortunate, nevertheless, that their service should be en-
listed in this practical task at the very moment when
they were becoming aware of the incapacity of abstract reason to negotiate that reconciliation between
custom and nature which they had so confidently
preached as the proper goal of human effort. It was
all very well for the philosophical tutor to say to the

[12] Condillac, *Oeuvres* (1798), XXI, 13.

young prince: "Religion and morality and politics should be based on natural law, they should be in harmony with the nature of man." The young prince, if he knew his philosophy, might very well reply: "The universe, I am told, is only matter in spontaneous motion, and man a mechanically determined product of nature; so that all things, just as they are —priests as well as philosophers, superstition as well as enlightenment, tyranny and the Inquisition as well as liberty and the *Encyclopédie*—are already in harmony with nature." What then? In that case the Philosopher would no doubt need to ameliorate abstract reason before he could ameliorate society. A society so obviously wrong could never be set right unless some distinction could be drawn between the custom that was naturally good and the custom that was naturally bad.

A distinction between good and bad! Not a novel idea, certainly; on the contrary, a very old, a most Christian idea. Must the Philosophers then fly, as Hume put it, to revealed truth? No, it was scarcely necessary to go as far as that; but it was necessary to execute a strategic retreat from the advanced position occupied by abstract reason, from the notion that nature has "no more regard to good above ill than to heat above cold." Otherwise, the campaign for a regenerated society was surely lost, and the great project for making dukes and peers useful no more than a dream. Rousseau understood this better than anyone else, perhaps because he understood it intuitively, without rationalistic inhibitions; and it was Rousseau who pointed out the lines along which the retreat must be made. Unless Philosophers

prescribe bounds to Nature, monsters, giants, pigmies and chimeras of all kinds might be specifically admitted into nature: every object would be disfigured, and we should have no common model of ourselves. I repeat it, in a picture of human nature, every figure should resemble man. . . . We should *distinguish between the variety in human nature and that which is essential to it.*[13]

Thus, the innate ideas which Locke had so politely dismissed by way of the hall door had to be surreptitiously brought back again through the kitchen window: the soul that Cartesian logic had eliminated from the individual had to be rediscovered in humanity. The soul of the individual might be evil, it might be temporary, it might even be an illusion. But the soul of humanity, this something "essential to" human nature, this "common model of ourselves" (and what was this but the old medieval "realism" come to life again?) was surely immortal because permanent and universal. What the Philosophers had to do, therefore, was to go up and down the wide world with the lamp of enlightenment looking, as Montaigne did before them, for "man in general." They had to identify and enumerate and de-

[13] *Eloise* (1810), I, 4.

scribe the qualities that were common to all men in order to determine what ideas and customs and institutions in their own time were out of harmony with the universal natural order. For the successful conduct of this enterprise, this eighteenth-century search for the Holy Grail, the light of abstract reason had to be supplemented by the light of experience. "Without history," said Priestley, "the advantages of our rational nature must have been rated very low."[14] It goes without saying that the history needed by the Philosophers was a "new history"—the history that would be philosophy teaching by example.

II

The "new history" is an old story. Since history is not an objective reality, but only an imaginative reconstruction of vanished events, the pattern that appears useful and agreeable to one generation is never entirely so to the next. There is thus a profound truth in Voltaire's witticism: "History is only a pack of tricks we play on the dead." It is unlikely that these tricks do the dead any harm, and it is certain that they do us much good. At best they help us to master our own difficulties; at worst they help us to endure them by nourishing the hope of a more resplendent future. The kind of tricks we play is therefore likely to depend on our attitude toward the pres-

[14] *Lectures on History and General Policy* (Am. ed., 1803), I, 52.

ent. If well enough satisfied with the present we are likely to pay our ancestors the doubtful compliment of approaching them with a studied and pedantic indifference; but when the times are out of joint we are disposed to blame them for it, or else we dress them up, as models suitable for us to imitate, in shining virtues which in fact they never possessed, which they would perhaps not have recognized as virtues at all.

We are all familiar with the "new history" of our own time. Two decades ago James Harvey Robinson plaintively deplored the time spent by historians in determining "whether Charles the Fat was at Ingelheim or Lustnau on July 1, 887"; suggested that they knew much about the past but little about man; and invited them, seeing that the times were so out of joint, to look more attentively at the jaw of the Heidelberg man—invited them, that is to say, to acquaint themselves with the "newer sciences of man" in order that they might "turn on the past and exploit it in the interests of advance."[15] Perhaps it is unnecessary to point out that Robinson was not the first of the newer historians. In the sixth century, under somewhat different circumstances, St. Augustine saw the advantages of a new history, and in fact created it by writing the *City of God,* which was undoubtedly one of the most ingenious and successful tricks ever played on the dead. At least it served its

[15] *The New History,* pp. 24, 70 ff., 81.

purpose well enough until the fifteenth and sixteenth centuries, when a new history was again called for. We then find humanists "exploiting the past" in the interest of classical learning, patriots in the interest of national or royal prestige, Protestants in the interest of the new religion, Catholics in the interest of the old faith. In the course of time, as religious and national hatreds subsided somewhat, the desire to exploit the past abated a little, and the seventeenth and early eighteenth centuries were proper times for historians to become erudite and uninspired—proper times for a Mabillon or a DuCange, for Bollandists and Benedictines, for many a meticulous researcher into the dead past, such, for example, as Fréret, whose innumerable memoirs printed in the Academy of Inscriptions make eighteen volumes of exact information which the world has willingly, and it may be usefully, forgotten.

Having examined some of the "orthodox" histories of that time, it does not surprise me to learn that the Philosophers were dissatisfied with them. They must have looked in vain for the "composition of the human heart" in the monographs of Fréret and the works of DeThou and Mézeray, while the something "essential to" human nature discovered by Bossuet in his *Discourse on Universal History* was certainly, from their point of view, quite the wrong thing. In the very accents, and almost in the very words, of James Harvey Robinson the Philosophers, therefore, raised the cry for a new history. Fénelon, although a Philosopher only by adoption, was no doubt one of the first. He complained that the "dry and sad maker of annals knows no other order than that of chronology," and thought it far more important to "observe the changes in the nation as a whole than to relate particular facts."[16] A voice crying in the wilderness, Fénelon's was; but toward the middle of the eighteenth century the cry became more insistent. Let us listen to a few of the Philosophers. Fontenelle: "To amass in the head fact upon fact, retain dates exactly, fill oneself with the spirit of wars, treaties of peace, marriages, genealogies—that is what is called knowing history. . . . I had as soon a man acquired exactly the history of all the clocks of Paris."[17] Grimm: "All the weight of our historians consists in a dull and pedantic discussion of facts which are commonly as unimportant as they are uncertain and disputed, and all their talent in refuting each other with a certain show of success." "History must be written by philosophers, whatever our pedants say."[18] Voltaire: "You prefer that philosophers should write ancient history because you wish to read it as a philosopher. You seek only useful truths, and have found, as you say, scarcely anything but useless errors."[19] Diderot: "Other historians relate

[16] *Oeuvres* (1848–51), VI, 639, 640.
[17] *Oeuvres* (1790), V, 433.
[18] *Correspondance littéraire*, III, 20; VI, 46.
[19] *Essai sur les moeurs* (1775), I, i.

facts to inform us of facts. You [Voltaire] relate them to excite in our hearts an intense hatred of lying, ignorance, hypocrisy, superstition, tyranny; and this anger remains even after the memory of the facts has disappeared."[20]

All Philosophers make the same complaint, that the "orthodox" historians accumulate facts for the sake of facts; all make the same demand, that the new history must be written by Philosophers in order to disengage from the facts those useful truths that will "lead us to a knowledge of ourselves and others."[21] Certainly, the demand did not go unheeded. During the latter half of the century Philosophers turned historians, or historians turned Philosophers, and between them these newer historians surveyed mankind from China to Peru. It was a favorite notion of the nineteenth-century historians that the eighteenth century was "antihistorical," that it was not interested in history since it desired to "break with the past" and start afresh. The assertion must involve a *non sequitur* in view of the extraordinary number of histories that were written, the number of editions they ran to, and the great importance attributed to the subject by all the leading men of the time. Names of famous and popular historians come to mind as soon as one stops to think: Gibbon, Hume, and Robertson; Rollin, Voltaire, Montes-

[20] *Oeuvres*, XIX, 460.
[21] Fontenelle, *Oeuvres* (1790), V, 431.

quieu, Mably, Raynal, and Herder. These are the better known names. One has only to run through Grimm's *Correspondance littéraire* to realize that in the later eighteenth century no subject was more read or written about than history. I say written about advisedly, because the Philosophers, whether they wrote history or not, almost all took the trouble to tell us why and how it ought to be written. And, without exception, so far as I know, they tell us that history, in connection with morality, is, of all subjects, one of the most important to be studied.

It may be that the Philosophers wished to "break with the past and start afresh." In a certain sense they did; but it does not follow that they were not interested in it. We may well be interested in the shackles that bind us, and that was just the sort of interest the Philosophers had in the past: they wished to learn why it was that men were still, after so many centuries of experience, bound by the follies and errors of their predecessors. Voltaire might say that "the history of great events in the world is scarcely more than a history of crimes";[22] but, for all that, he gave himself the trouble of writing a history of the world in six volumes. No one thought less well of the past than Chastellux, who was convinced that existing ideas and customs were little more than a mass of acquired ignorance. In order to be happy, he said, there is "far greater need of forgetting than of

[22] *Essai*, I, 172.

remembering," since the great object of enlightened men should be to "raise the edifice of Reason on the ruins of opinion." As a contribution to this great object he wrote a two-volume general history entitled *De la félicité publique*. The public happiness was something to be attained in the future; it could not be attained without breaking with the past; but in order to induce men to break with the past it was first of all necessary to show them how bad it was. Thus it turned out that in writing a book on *la félicité publique* Chastellux found that he had assumed the obligation, as he put it, of "retracing the unhappiness of humanity."[23]

Even Chastellux did not write history merely in order to show how bad the past was. It would be useless, he said, to write the history of so many particular events if from them "we were unable to disengage general facts . . . far more certain than those which have been so carefully transmitted to us."[24] Not all Philosophers thought so badly of the past as Chastellux, but they all shared his view that history should be studied in order to disengage those "general facts" that might serve as useful lessons. On this point one might quote from the writings of men as different as Fontenelle, Priestley, Bolingbroke, Condillac, Gibbon, Rousseau, and Rollin. But it would be useless; their views are but variations on a single

[23] *De la félicité publique* (1822), I, 220.
[24] *Ibid.*, p. 55.

theme and this theme is nowhere better stated than in the Preface to Duclos' *Histoire de Louis XI*.

> I shall not undertake to prove the utility of history: it is a truth too generally recognized to need proof. . . . We see on the theater of the world a certain number of scenes which succeed each other in endless repetition: where we see the same faults followed regularly by the same misfortunes, we may reasonably think that if we could have known the first we might have avoided the others. The past should enlighten us on the future: knowledge of history is no more than an anticipated experience.

And, finally, let Hume put the sum and substance of the matter in two sentences: "Mankind are so much the same, in all times and places, that history informs us of nothing new or strange in this particular. Its chief use is only to discover the constant and universal principles of human nature."[25]

Did the Philosophers, then, wish, as the nineteenth-century historians liked to think, to "break with the past"? Obviously, they wished to get rid of the bad ideas and customs inherited from the past; quite as obviously they wished to hold fast to the good ones, if any good ones there were. But the question is worth answering only because it is not a proper question to ask; and it is an improper question to ask because it projects into that climate of opinion a preconception that was in fact not there.

[25] *Essays*, II, 94.

The phrase "break with the past" came spontaneously to the lips of nineteenth-century historians because they were so much concerned with the "continuity of history," the evolution of institutions. After twenty-five years of revolution and international war, most people felt the need of stabilizing society; and the most satisfactory rationalization of this need was presented by those historians and jurists who occupied themselves with social origins, who asked the question, How did society, especially the particular society of this or that nation, come to be what it is? The unconscious preconception involved in this question was that if men understood just how the customs of any nation had come to be what they were, they would sufficiently realize the folly of trying to refashion them all at once according to some rational plan. Nineteenth-century historians and jurists, therefore, established the continuity of history: to suppose it possible to break the continuity of history naturally seemed to them "unhistorical"; and the attempt to do so as disastrous as it would be for a flourishing tree to break with the roots that nourished it.

But the conception of continuity was of little use to the eighteenth-century Philosophers. No doubt, the idea was there, ready to be picked up and made use of, if any one had needed it. It was implied in the notion that the moderns are superior to the ancients because they profit by ancient experience and knowl-

edge. It was implied in the shining vision of perfectibility. It is to be found in the writings of Vico,
Grimm, Turgot, Diderot, Herder, Montesquieu, and
Leibnitz. Diderot stumbled over all the elements essential to the Darwinian theory of evolution; but the
point is that he stumbled over them as if they were
obstacles instead of stepping-stones, as for him, indeed, they were. Professor Vaughan points out that
Montesquieu was troubled with difficulties which the
idea of the progressive unfolding of institutions
would easily have disposed of, and is at a loss to understand why Montesquieu did not make use of the
idea, since all the elements of it were there, in his
own manuscript, staring up at him from the table.
Very true it is that the idea was there in his own
manuscript. But the significant thing is that Montesquieu made little use of it, that no one (Leibnitz excepted) made much use of it. The idea was present
in the eighteenth century, but no one made it welcome; it wandered forlornly about in the fringes of
consciousness, it timidly approached the threshold,
but it never really got across.

The reason is that the eighteenth-century Philosophers were not primarily interested in stabilizing society, but in changing it. They did not ask how society had come to be what it was, but how it could be
made better than it was. There is no more apt illus-
tration of this slant of mind than the famous opening
sentences of Rousseau's *Social Contract*. "Man is

born free, and is everywhere in chains. How was this change made? *I do not know*. What can make it legitimate? I believe I can answer that question." Do not, therefore, ask the Philosophers that question so dear to the nineteenth century: "How did society come to be what it is?" Almost without exception they will reply with Rousseau: "We do not know." And we at once feel that they have it on the tip of their tongues to dismiss us with an impatient, "and we do not care." What difference does it make, they seem to be saying, how society came to be what it is? There it is for all men to see, obviously irrational, oppressive, unjust, obviously contrary to the essential nature of man, obviously needing to be set right, and that speedily. What we seek to know is how it may be set right; and we look to the past for light, not on the origins of society, but on its future state. We wish neither to break with the past nor to hold fast to it, but to make use of it: we wish to disengage from it those ideas, customs, and institutions which are so widely distributed and so persistent in human experience that they may be regarded as embodying those "constant and universal principles of human nature" upon which we may rely for establishing a more equitable *régime* than that which now exists.

In the light of this preconception we can read the philosopher-historians without being bored or annoyed. Since they were not primarily concerned with continuity, with the evolution, the unfolding, the differentiation of institutions, they could afford to be loftily contemptuous of "mere events," and were under no compulsion of conscience to lavish loving care upon the determination of the exact date. They were looking for "man in general," and it is unreasonable of us to be annoyed because they did not look for him at Ingelheim or Lustnau on July 1, 887. Man in general, like the economic man, was a being that did not exist in the world of time and place, but in the conceptual world, and he could therefore be found only by abstracting from all men in all times and all places those qualities which all men shared. No doubt Charles the Fat, being, like Socrates, a man, might exhibit at Ingelheim or Lustnau some of the qualities he shared with Socrates. The important point was to note those qualities as exhibited: it mattered not whether they were exhibited at Ingelheim or at Lustnau, whether on July 1 or on some other day, the exact time and place being no more than temporal "accidents" useful chiefly for illustrative purposes.

Obviously, therefore, the chronological order was not essential to the writing of history thus conceived. It might, indeed, be adopted as the most convenient order, and, in fact, we find Hume, Gibbon, Voltaire, and Mably presenting their material more or less in this order. But a philosopher-historian might equally well ignore the chronological order, as Montesquieu and Raynal did, without laying himself open to the charge of being no historian. The method adopted by Montesquieu would seem to be *the* method for the philosopher-historian, the ideal method. For the task of the philosopher-historian, theoretically speaking, was to note the ideas, customs, and institutions of all peoples at all times and in all places, to put them side by side, and to cancel out as it were those that appeared to be merely local or temporary: what remained would be those that were common to humanity. From these common aspects of human experience it would then be possible, if at all, to discover, as Hume put it, the "constant and universal principles of human nature" and on these principles to base a reconstructed society. The ideal method for the philosopher-historian would thus be the comparative method, the strictly objective, inductive, scientific method.

Nevertheless, this ideal method was not employed by the Philosophers, not even by Montesquieu, who made the bravest appearance of doing so. It is, indeed, highly illuminating that those parts of the *Esprit des lois* in which Montesquieu was most successful in applying the comparative and inductive method, those parts in which he was most objective and scientific, were precisely the parts that pleased the Philosophers least. Generally speaking, the *Esprit des lois* left a bad taste in the mouths of the Philosophers because Montesquieu insisted that the "constant and universal principles of human nature" were after all "relative," so that, for example, what was suited to the nature of man in certain climates might very well be unsuited to the nature of man in other climates. The Philosophers felt that Montesquieu was too much enamored of facts as such to treat certain facts as harshly as they deserved, and it shocked them to see him dallying lightly with episodes that were no better than they should be. Voltaire (Voltaire of all people!) criticized Montesquieu for his *levity,* for being more disposed to astonish than to instruct his readers, and thought it monstrous that feudal kings and barons should be called "our fathers." According to Condorcet, Montesquieu would have done better if he had not been "more occupied with finding the reasons for that which is than with seeking that which ought to be."[26] And even Rousseau, who admired Montesquieu more than the others did, finds that he, like Grotius before him, is too much inclined to establish the right by the fact.[27] It is surely a paradox needing explanation that the Philosophers, who professed to study history in order to establish the rights suitable to man's nature on the facts of human experience, should have denounced Montesquieu precisely because he was too much inclined to establish the right by the fact. Is it, then, possible that the Philosophers were not really

[26] *Oeuvres* (1847), VIII, 188.
[27] *Political Writings of Rousseau* (Vaughan ed.), II, 147.

interested in establishing the rights suitable to man's nature on the facts of human experience? Is it possible that they were engaged in that nefarious medieval enterprise of reconciling the facts of human experience with truths already, in some fashion, revealed to them?

III

Alas yes, that is, indeed, the fact! The eighteenth-century Philosophers, like the medieval scholastics, held fast to a revealed body of knowledge, and they were unwilling or unable to learn anything from history which could not, by some ingenious trick played on the dead, be reconciled with their faith. Their faith, like the faith by which any age lives, was born of their experience and their needs; and since their experience and their needs were in deadly conflict with the traditional and established and still powerful philosophy of church and state, the articles of their faith were at every point opposed to those of the established philosophy. The essential articles of the religion of the Enlightenment may be stated thus: (1) man is not natively depraved; (2) the end of life is life itself, the good life on earth instead of the beatific life after death; (3) man is capable, guided solely by the light of reason and experience, of perfecting the good life on earth; and (4) the first and essential condition of the good life on earth is the freeing of men's minds from the bonds of ignorance and superstition, and of their bodies from the arbitrary oppression of the constituted social authorities. With this creed the "constant and universal principles of human nature," which Hume tells us are to be discovered by a study of history, must be in accord, and "man in general" must be a creature who would conveniently illustrate these principles. What these "universal principles" were the Philosophers, therefore, understood before they went in search of them, and with "man in general" they were well acquainted, having created him in their own image. They knew instinctively that "man in general" is natively good, easily enlightened, disposed to follow reason and common sense; generous and humane and tolerant, more easily led by persuasion than compelled by force; above all a good citizen and a man of virtue, being well aware that, since the rights claimed by himself are only the natural and imprescriptible rights of all men, it is necessary for him voluntarily to assume the obligations and to submit to the restraints imposed by a just government for the commonweal.

It is apparent that, in professing with so disarming an air of candor to be studying history in order to discover the constant and universal principles of human nature, they are deceiving us, these philosopher-historians. But we can easily forgive them for that, since they are, even more effectively, deceiving themselves. They do not know that the "man in general" they are looking for is just their own image, that the principles they are bound to find are the very ones they start out with. That is the trick they play on the dead. They unconsciously give themselves away by their insistence on the union of morality and politics. Those who would separate morality and politics, according to Rousseau, know nothing of either. "History is good for nothing," said Fontenelle, "if it be not united with morality. . . . It is certain that one may know all that men ever did and still be ignorant of man himself."[28] In the Preface to his great work Montesquieu tells us that the "facts" meant nothing to him until he discovered the principles which they were to illustrate. "I have many times begun and many times abandoned this work; I have repeatedly thrown away the sheets already written; . . . I followed my object without forming any design: I was unable to grasp either the rules or the exceptions; I found the truth only to lose it: but when I discovered my principles, everything I sought came to me." And Diderot: "Some may think that a knowledge of history should precede that of morality: I am not of that opinion: it seems to me more useful and expedient to possess the idea of the just and the unjust before possessing a knowledge of the actions and the men to whom one ought to apply it."[29] It is only too clear: the philosopher-historians possess the idea of the just and the unjust, they have their "universal

[28] *Oeuvres*, V, 434, 435.   [29] *Oeuvres*, III, 493.

principles" and their "man in general" well in hand before they start out to explore the field of human experience.

They start out, under the banner of objectivity and with a flourish of scholarly trumpets, as if on a voyage of discovery in unknown lands. They start out, but in a very real sense they never pass the frontiers of the eighteenth century, never really enter the country of the past or of distant lands. They cannot afford to leave the battlefield of the present where they are so fully engaged in a life-and-death struggle with Christian philosophy and the infamous things that support it—superstition, intolerance, tyranny. Against the enemy they have brought to bear all the resources of reason and common sense; but the enemy is still firmly entrenched all about them, and reason and common sense, redoubtable as they may be, are in need of assistance. This assistance the Philosophers profess to be seeking in the facts of human history; but, in truth, they are only executing a flank movement in order to enlarge the field of battle, in order to deliver their attack from a more elevated position. They project the conflict into the centuries so that it may be regarded as something more than an eighteenth-century squabble between Philosophers and priests, so that it may be regarded as an aspect of a conflict exemplified in all human experience, the conflict between the cosmic forces of good and evil, between the City of Light and the

City of Darkness—the eternal conflict for the soul of man. Reason and common sense have noted the evil character of Christian philosophy; it will be history's function to exhibit it in action, to note the striking examples of its evil influence.

The philosopher-historians were very sure that all human experience would justify reason and common sense; but, in order that it should turn out so, it was necessary for them to distribute, over the picture of the past, the appropriate lights and shadows. It was necessary for them to appeal, as one may say, from history drunk to history sober, to differentiate between the good times and the bad times. The bad times to be condemned as contrary to reason and common sense were obviously just those Dark Ages of ignorance and superstition and tyranny when Christian philosophy exercised undisputed sway; and no extended research was required to find the happier eras of mankind which might be set, in shining, instructive contrast, over against the Dark Ages. There were, first, the two golden ages of Pericles and Augustus. The Philosophers had all (or nearly all) read the classical authors in college (as often as not under Jesuit or Benedictine instructors!); and they had learned from classical writers, or from Rollin's rehash of classical historians, or from Plutarch (above all from Plutarch), or from the didactic "asides" of the translators and editors of Plutarch, what classical heroes to model themselves upon,

what Spartan or Roman virtues to emulate.[80] And
there was the "rebirth" after the Dark Ages as well
as the golden ages before them; and it was a matter
of common knowledge that the age of Louis XIV and
of the eighteenth century had added something to the
light and learning, the liberty and virtue, of the ancient world and of the Renaissance: so that the philosopher-historians had at their disposal what Voltaire called the *"quatre âges heureux"* to set over
against the Dark Ages when Christian philosophy
had fastened like a blight upon the human spirit.
Fortunately, there was more than this. Human experience could no longer be limited to the Mediter-
ranean lands, nor history to the European tradition.
To say nothing of the happier experience of England
and her American colonies, there was the experience
of non-Christian peoples in distant lands—in Asia
and the two Indies; and from the accounts of six-
teenth- and seventeenth-century travelers it was
made clear that far the greater part of mankind,
during far the greater period of recorded history, had
lived (except, indeed, when oppressed and corrupted
by Christian powers) more happily and humanely,
under laws and customs more free and equitable, and
more in accord with natural religion and morality,
than the peoples of Europe had done during the cen-

[80] For much of the detailed information on which this statement is based, I am indebted to the researches of Mr. H. T. Parker,
formerly a graduate student in Cornell University.

turies of ecclesiastical ascendancy. All these happier times and peoples the philosopher-historians mobilized in the service of reason and common sense: the testimony of the *quatre âges heureux*, of the English, of "our brave Americans," of the "wise Chinese," the "noble Indian," the "good savages"—all this convincing testimony could now happily be turned against the Christian centuries to refute and confound them.

This was the function of the new history: to make that distinction, which abstract reason was unable to make, between the naturally good and the naturally bad, between the customs that were suited and those that were unsuited to man's nature. Human experience would confirm the verdict of reason, that Christian philosophy and the infamous things that supported it were inimical to the welfare of mankind. I wish now, in conclusion, to note very briefly how certain historians, by different methods, managed to "turn on the past and exploit it" in the interest of this fundamental need.

Let us take first two very popular histories, Mably's history of France and Hume's history of England. The first thing to note about Mably's history of France is that it is not a history of France, but *Observations on the History of France*. And, in fact, what Mably observes is that long ago, in the time of Charlemagne, the French possessed the elements of a political constitution suited to the genius of the na-

tion, but that subsequently, in the centuries of feudal anarchy and ecclesiastical and "ministerial despotism," this constitution was overlaid by customs
unsuited to the French people; and the purpose of
Mably's volumes is to disengage this proper constitution from the rubbish heap of accumulated custom,
and to show his contemporaries how it might easily
be refurbished and made use of now that the French
were sufficiently enlightened to know what they were
doing. Hume's history is less narrowly and less ex-
plicitly didactic than Mably's. At first reading it
seems no more than a dull and colorless chronicle of
events, and one wonders why it should have been so
eagerly read by a generation that expected its historians to substitute for the narrative of events a description of *les moeurs*. On more attentive reading
the reason for its popularity is clear. Hume managed, with unobtrusive skill, to weave into the tex-
ture of the narrative a condemnation of the very
things the eighteenth century wanted condemned—
tyranny, superstition, intolerance. The story is a narrative of events, but it is after all well told, and
above all told *en philosophe:* that is to say, not in
order to trace the evolution of events or to explain
them in terms of their origins and effects, but in order to apply to events the "idea of the just and the
unjust," in order to apply to them the ready-made
judgments of the age of reason. It would be a dull
reader indeed who could not carry away from such a

book that most useful of lessons for the eighteenth century, namely, that, *except* for the ambition of princes and politicians, the worldly interests and intrigues of priests, the emotional excesses of fanatics, and the fears of a superstitious and degraded populace—*except* for these recognized and remediable evils, the history of England might have been what the history of any people ought to be.

Let us now look at three works in some sense universal, or at least international, in their scope—the works of Raynal, Voltaire, and Montesquieu. Raynal's book, *The Philosophical and Political History of the Indies,* half fiction though it may be, is of interest to us because of its great popularity. Revised three times, it ran to fifty-four editions before the end of the century,[31] and Horace Walpole not inaptly, allowance being made for the exaggeration of a phrase maker, called it the "Bible of two worlds." The work was welcomed because it was a compendium in which the reader could find the gist, appropriately elaborated in a philosophical manner, of what the travelers and explorers had said about the "wise Chinese" and the "good savages." Raynal took his readers (very conveniently for them, since they could join or leave the expedition at any point) on the "grand tour" through the non-Christian world; and like a good Cook's guide he showed them what

[31] *Journal of Modern History,* III, 576.

was admirable in the native customs of these foreign peoples, and especially what corruptions and miseries, imposed upon them by their Christian conquerors, a Philosopher should note and deplore. Raynal was less subtle than the author of the *Lettres persanes;* but of all the books which condemned the artificial and Christian civilization of Europe by contrasting it with the natural virtues of primitive peoples, *The Philosophical and Political History of the Indies* was best suited to the needs of the average reader, and for that reason was undoubtedly the most influential.

Of Voltaire's great work, the *Essai sur les moeurs,* little need be said. Like Wells's *Outline of History,* it was a general history from the earliest known times written to point a moral: to show that the history of great events in the world is scarcely more than a history of crimes; that the Dark Ages of human experience were precisely those when men were most dominated by the Christian church; and that almost the only times of light and learning, of progress in the arts and sciences, were the *quatre âges heureux* when the evils of priestcraft were somewhat abated and the minds of men were in consequence somewhat free to follow reason. No doubt there is more in the *Essai* than this; but this is the chief "lesson" which the eighteenth-century reader was likely to learn from it. Its primary effect, as Diderot said, was to excite in the hearts of the readers "an intense hatred of lying, ignorance, hypocrisy, superstition, and tyranny."

Montesquieu's *Esprit des lois* calls for a somewhat more extended comment, since it has been defaced by the misleading glosses of nineteenth-century interpreters. Very much as the Philosophers "adopted" Fénelon and made use of him to refute Bossuet, nineteenth-century writers adopted Montesquieu and made use of him to refute the Philosophers. They created a Montesquieu in their own image, making him a forerunner of the objective, scientific historians, primarily interested in the facts, primarily concerned to establish, by the inductive and comparative method, the "relativity" of institutions and the hopeless dependence of custom on climate and geography. The Philosophers themselves, as we have seen, suspected Montesquieu of being too much occupied with finding the reasons for that which is, too much inclined to establish the right by the fact. There is some truth in all this, and by carefully selecting certain passages and certain books in the *Esprit des lois* one can prove a great deal. Professor Vaughan tells us that in "the last five books" Montesquieu is the historian whose one care is "to ascertain the facts and to explain how and why each of them arose."[32] It may be so. But after all what are five books in the sight of Montesquieu who can make

[32] *Studies in the History of Political Philosophy*, I, 275.

a chapter out of one sentence? What are five books out of thirty-one? And Professor Vaughan really excludes one of the five, leaving only four. Very well, let us except these four books, and any passages like them elsewhere; and let us admit that in so far Montesquieu is the "pure historian," whose only care is to "ascertain the facts."

But then let us read the rest of the work, first blotting out the innumerable "Books" and "Chapters" and their numbers; and let us remember as we read that the work was written by Montesquieu, not by a nineteenth-century historian or professional student of comparative politics, but by an eighteenth-century aristocrat and man of affairs, *M. le Président à Mortier,* a man of shrewd practical sense who had read widely, who had long reflected on the problems of man and his world, and who liked to set down his reflections and to support and illustrate them by such pat instances as "came to him" from his experience or his reading. If we read the *Esprit des lois* so, I think we shall understand that what we are reading is not a systematic treatise on politics (everyone has noted the fact that it is not systematic), but a book of disconnected reflections—a book of essays really. It may then occur to us that the author is in some sense the eighteenth-century Montaigne—Montaigne with a pinch of Bayle added, and with something else added, some strain of eighteenth-century discontent with things as they are, and of the eighteenth-century impulse to set them right. We shall at all events be astonished that Condorcet could think Montesquieu too much occupied with that which is, too little with that which ought to be. Information about that which is, Montesquieu took as it came to him—from classical writers, from reports of travelers, from oral tradition. The information is often enough extremely superficial, and so rarely questioned that for reliable knowledge of the facts one goes rather to Voltaire, to say nothing of Gibbon. Montesquieu has little reverence for the facts as such; for him they are not fundamental but illustrative, their essential truth is not in themselves but in their implications; they are (whether noted with careful accuracy does not greatly matter) the conveniently possible incidents which make concrete and vivid the general policies proper to this or that kind of government, the general maxims which any ruler *ought to* follow under such and such circumstances. That little word "ought"—what a fundamental rôle it plays in the *Esprit des lois!* Open the book anywhere: "Religion and civil law *ought* to have a tendency to make men good citizens."[33] The laws of chastity "arise from those of nature, and *ought to be* respected in all nations."[34] The political and civil laws "of each nation *ought to be* no more than special applications of the law of human rea-

[33] Bk. XXIV, chap. xiv.   [34] Bk. XV, chap. xii.

son."[85] Although the principle of a republic is virtue, "this does not mean that in any particular republic the people are virtuous, but that they *ought to be* so."[86] One might go on indefinitely. It is too obvious to be missed, and over against the judgment of Condorcet we must set the more just judgment of D'Alembert: "He occupies himself less with laws that have been made than with those that ought to be made."[87]

Before estimating a book it is well to read its title with care. And what is the title of Montesquieu's book? Not *the laws,* but *the spirit* of the laws. Montesquieu was not primarily concerned with the laws as they exist, but with some ideal quality of rightness which, considering all the physical and human circumstances, they ought to have. For those who seek, by the inductive method, to establish a science of politics on the "facts" of human experience, there is very little in the *Esprit des lois.* But where could the eighteenth-century reformer, bent on sapping the foundations of church and state in the *ancien régime,* find an arsenal better equipped with ammunition for his purpose? Where could he find the cause of constitutional government in France more effectively set forth, more solidly grounded on "universal principles"? Where could he find a greater variety of facts, analogies, contrasts, indirect refutations, sly

[85] Bk. I, chap. iii.   [86] Bk. III, chap. xi.
[87] *Oeuvres* (1821), III, 450.

left-handed compliments and suave, ironical obei-
sances—all subtly designed to make the dogmas and
the practices of the "one true" and "revealed" religion ridiculous? Nowhere, I venture to say. Montesquieu himself has told us what to think of his work,
in telling us what "the wisest and most enlightened"
men of his own time thought of it: "They have regarded the *Esprit des lois* as a useful work; they
have thought its morality sound, its principles just;
that it was well designed to make good citizens; to
refute pernicious opinions, to encourage good ones."[38]

And the great Gibbon? Gibbon, so often bracketed
with Thucydides and Tacitus as a model historian, so
impeccable in his scholarship, so objective, so *appar-
ently* objective, so accurate at all events in his statement of facts—what of him? Simply this: That it
was Gibbon after all who sought out the enemy in
his stronghold and made the direct frontal attack on
the Christian centuries. Among the "ruins of the
Capitol" he first conceived the project of narrating
the decline and fall of the Roman Empire, "the
greatest, perhaps, and the most awful scene in the
history of mankind." For twenty years he labored at
his self-imposed task. And with what skill, with
what a wealth of precise and accurate detail he tells
the story of the fall of civilization from that high
point in the second century, the "most happy and
prosperous" in the annals of mankind. With what

[38] *Défense de l'esprit des lois,* Part II.

tolerant and amused, and yet saddened and resigned, aloofness he writes of people whom he disliked, of activities he deplored. With what relief he returns, on those rare occasions when his subject permits, to "breathe the pure and vigorous air of the Republic." With what urbanity, with what grave and lofty irony and learned misunderstanding this enlightened *savant* describes the spread and triumph of Christianity, reargues the subtle dialectical disputes concerning the Trinity and the Incarnation, and relates the childish activities of Stylites and the "monkish saints" —innumerable "transactions" which, being alike "scandalous for the Church and pernicious to the State," could not fail to excite the "contempt and pity" of a Philosopher. In the pages of the *Decline and Fall*, we seem to be taking a long journey, but all the time we remain in one place: we sit with Gibbon in the ruins of the Capitol. It is from the ruins of the Capitol that we perceive, as from a great distance, a thousand years filled with dim shapes of men moving blindly, performing strangely, in an unreal shadowy world. We do not enter the Middle Ages, or relive a span of human experience: still we sit in the ruins of the Capitol, becoming cramped and half numb listening, all this long stationary time, to our unwearied guide as he narrates for us, in a melancholy and falling cadence, the disaster that mankind has suffered, the defeat inflicted by the forces of evil on the human spirit. The *Decline and Fall* is a history, yes; but something more than a history, a memorial oration: Gibbon is commemorating the death of ancient civilization; he has described, for the "instruction of future ages," the "triumph of barbarism and religion."

The triumph of barbarism and religion! The words fittingly call up the past as imagined by the philosophical century. It was as if mankind, betrayed by barbarism and religion, had been expelled from nature's Garden of Eden. The Christian Middle Ages were the unhappy times after the fall and expulsion, the unfruitful, probationary centuries when mankind, corrupted and degraded by error, wandered blindly under the yoke of oppression. But mankind has at last emerged, or is emerging, from the dark wilderness of the past into the bright, ordered world of the eighteenth century. From this high point of the eighteenth century the Philosophers survey the past and anticipate the future. They recall the miseries and errors of the past as mature men recall the difficulties and follies of youth, with bitter memories it may be, yet with a tolerant smile after all, with a sigh of satisfaction and a complacent feeling of assurance: the present is so much better than the past. But the future, what of that? Since the present is so much better than the past, will not the future be much better than the present? To the future the Philosophers therefore look, as to a promised land, a new millennium.

IV

The Uses of Posterity

La postérité pour le philosophe, c'est l'autre monde de l'homme religieux. DIDEROT.

Whatever was the beginning of this world, the end will be glorious and paradisaical, beyond what our imagination can now conceive. PRIESTLEY.

I

PAST and future are two time regions which we commonly separate by a third which we call the present. But strictly speaking the present does not exist, or is at best no more than an infinitesimal point in time, gone before we can note it as present. Nevertheless we must have a present; and so we get one by robbing the past, by holding on to the most recent events and pretending that they all belong to our immediate perceptions. If, for example, I raise my arm, the total event is a series of occurrences of which the first are past before the last have taken place; yet I perceive it as a single movement executed in one instant of time. This telescoping of successive occurrences into one present moment, Philosophers call the "specious present." Just what limits they would assign to the specious present I do not know; but I will make a free use of it, and say for convenience that we can extend the specious present as much as we like. In common speech we do so: we speak of the "present hour," the "present year," the "present generation." Perhaps all living creatures have a specious present; but no doubt what chiefly distinguishes man from other animals is that his specious present may be deliberately and purposefully enlarged and diversified and enriched. The extent to which it may be thus enlarged and enriched will obviously depend on knowledge (the artificial extension of memory) of the past and of distant places; so that the educated man may, whenever he wishes, bring into consciousness a general image (sketchy and incorrect in detail though it may be) of the long past of mankind and hold it there, making it for the time being a part of his "present."

The normal and sensible man does not often drag the whole past of mankind into the present. But at any moment of deliberate and purposeful activity each one of us brings into present consciousness a certain part of the past, such actual or artificial memories of past events as may be necessary to orient us in our little world of endeavor. To be oriented we must be prepared for what is coming to us, and to be prepared for what is coming to us it is necessary not only to recall certain past events but to anticipate (note I do not say "predict") the future. Thus, from the specious present, which always includes more or less of the past, the future refuses to be excluded; and the more of the past we drag into the specious present, the more a hypothetical, patterned future crowds into it also. If our memories of past events are short and barren, our anticipations of future events will be short and barren; if our memories are rich and diversified, our anticipations of what is to come are likely to be more or less so, too. But the main point is that the character of the pattern of the one, no less than its richness and extent, will depend on the character of the other. Which comes first, which is cause and which effect, whether our memories construct a pattern of past events at the behest of our desires and hopes, or whether our desires and hopes spring from a pattern of past events imposed upon us by experience and knowledge, I shall not attempt to say. What I suspect is that memory of past and anticipation of future events work together, go hand in hand in a friendly way, without disputing over priority and leadership. Be that as it may, they go together, so that in a real sense the specious present as held in consciousness at any time is a pattern of thought woven instantaneously from the threads of memories, perceptions, and anticipations.

If this be true of the individual mind in its ordinary functioning, is it not also true of that generalized "mind" of an epoch or climate of opinion which we courageously construct for purposes of scholastic discussion? Let us, at all events, adopt that hypothesis. We may find it useful to assume that there was an eighteenth-century "mind," and to suppose that it had, like an individual mind, a specious present composed of its memories of the past, its perceptions of present occurrences, and its anticipations of future events. In the last lecture I endeavored to show how this eighteenth-century mind, as reflected in the writings of the Philosophers, recalled the past as a period of ignorance and unhappiness from which men had emerged into a present that was clearly better. In this lecture I shall endeavor to show how these memories and present perceptions disposed the eighteenth-century mind to look forward to the future as to a promised land, a kind of utopia.

I have already stated, more than once perhaps, that the Philosophers were not professional philosophers sitting in cool ivory towers for contemplative purposes only, but crusaders whose mission it was to recover the holy places of the religion of humanity from Christian philosophy and the infamous things that supported it. The directing impulse of their thought was that mankind had been corrupted and betrayed by false doctrines. Their essential task was to destroy these false doctrines; and in order to do so they had of course to meet the doctrines of Christian philosophy with opposed doctrines, contrary ideas. But not with radically different ideas, not with ideas of a different order altogether, since it is true of ideas, as of men, that they cannot fight unless they occupy the same ground: ideas that rush toward each other on different levels of apprehension will pass without conflict or mutual injury because they never establish contact, never collide. In order to defeat Christian philosophy the Philosophers had therefore to meet it on the level of certain common preconceptions. They could never rout the enemy by denying that human life is a significant drama—the notion was too widely, too unconsciously held, even by the Philosophers themselves, for that; but, admitting that human life is significant drama, the Philosophers could claim that the Christian version of the drama was a false and pernicious one; and their best hope of displacing the Christian version lay in recasting it, and in bringing it up to date. In short, the task of the Philosophers was to present another interpretation of the past, the present, and the future state of mankind.

In presenting a new version of the drama of human life, the Philosophers were employing tactics which Christian theologians had themselves employed long ago. The early Christian writers had won their battle, in so far as they did win it, by adapting to the needs and experience of the ancient world (which, like the eighteenth century, needed to be set right) the old Greek theme of cyclical decline and recovery. The classical idea of a golden age, or situation created by some happily inspired Lycurgus or Solon, the Christian theologians reinterpreted in terms of their own biblical story. They gave an added glamor to the golden age by pushing it back to the beginning of things, to the creation of man and his world; they made it seem more real, more authentic, by placing it historically—in the Garden of Eden; and they endowed it with perfection and authority by transforming the inspired legislator into the one true and omniscient and benevolent God. But however right things may have been in the golden age or the Garden of Eden, there had been a decline and fall from that happy first state. Classical writers (with some exceptions) regarded the present state of man as a natural degeneration, effected by fate and human frailty, and they could look forward to nothing better than some fortunate chance, the reappearance of the inspired legislator or philosopher-king, to set things right again, and beyond that to another inevitable falling away: so that, since "time is the enemy of man," human history appeared to them to be no more than an endless series of cycles, an eternal repetition of the familiar phenomena of recovery and degeneration. According to Marcus Aurelius, the rational soul

goeth about the whole universe and the void surrounding it and traces its plan, and stretches forth into the infinitude of Time, and comprehends the cyclical Regeneration of all things, and takes stock of it and discerns that our children will see nothing fresh, just as our fathers too never saw anything more than we. So that in a manner the man of forty years, if he have a grain of sense, in view of this sameness has seen all that has been and shall be.[1]

The classical version of human life was dramatic enough, but its dramatic quality lay in the implication that human life is ordered by an implacable fate from which there is no escape: it was a drama without a happy ending, or any ending at all. This was no doubt its fatal weakness. The rational soul, at the age of forty years, might find a pale satisfaction in traversing infinite time only to learn that there was nothing new under the sun, and never would be; but the common run of men, finding the brief span of life harsh and profitless and precarious, wanted compensations for unhappiness, the joy, at the very least, of looking forward with hope: common men wanted the play to have a happy ending. The Christian version, written for common men, provided the happy ending which they wanted. The Christian version did not make the present life of men less unhappy, or less fatefully determined, but it presented a more intelligible, a far more agreeable interpretation of it. The "fall of man" was more easily understood when it could be attributed to a definite first act of disobedience to the paternal authority of God; and present miseries and martyrdoms became endurable, became high virtues even, when thought to be

[1] *The Communings with Himself of Marcus Aurelius Antoninus*, trans. C. R. Haines (1916), XI, sec. 1.

inflicted as punishments that might prove to be the price of eternal felicity in heaven. The Christian version put an end to the helpless, hopeless world by substituting for the eternal "nothing new" another world altogether new, a golden age to come in place of a golden age past and done with; it called on the future to redress the balance of the present, and required of the individual man, as a condition of entering the promised land, nothing but the exercise of those negative virtues which common men understood so well—the virtues of resignation and obedience.

The extraordinary sway which the Christian story exercised over the minds of men is easily understood. No interpretation of the life of mankind ever more exactly reflected the experience, or more effectively responded to the hopes of average men. To be aware of present trials and misfortunes, to look back with fond memories to the happier times (imagined so at least) of youth, to look forward with hope to a more serene and secure old age—what could more adequately sum up the experience of the great majority? And what was the Christian story if not an application of this familiar individual experience to the life of mankind? Mankind had its youth, its happier time in the Garden of Eden, to look back upon, its present middle period of misfortunes to endure, its future security to hope for. The average man needed no theology to understand universal experi-

ence when presented in terms so familiar; and it con-
soled him—it no doubt added something to his sense
of personal significance—to realize that his own life,
however barren and limited it might be, was but a
concrete exemplification of the experience which God
had decreed for all the generations of men. But better than all that—best of all—he could understand
that there should sometime be an end made, a judgment pronounced upon the world of men and things,
a day of reckoning in which evil men would be pun-
ished and good men rewarded: he could believe that
with all his heart, with a conviction fortified by the
stored-up memories of the injustices he had witnessed, the unmerited injuries he had suffered. The
average man could believe all that; and in the measure that he could believe it he could hope, he could
so easily convince himself, that in that last day he
would be found among those judged good, .among
those to be admitted into that other world in which
things would be forever right.

Superficially considered, considered as an account
of events historically verifiable, the story was no
doubt flimsy enough; and the mere increase of
knowledge—knowledge of the classical world, of the
early history of the church, of remote primitive and
non-Christian peoples—had done much to discredit
it. Since the fifteenth century, or even earlier, the
Humanists, fascinated by the newly discovered past,
had substituted for the Garden of Eden the golden

age of classical civilization, just as the Christian theologians had in their time substituted the Garden of Eden for the golden age of Greek imagination. This was all very well as an initial method of attack: it was a good thing, and even necessary, for the Humanists to go to school to the Greeks and Romans, to learn all that they knew, even for a time to imitate them as models as yet unsurpassed: an excellent device all this was for throwing fresh light on the origins of the Christian story, and on the drab and dreary learning which, in the course of centuries, had overlaid and obscured its essential meaning. But the tenacious strength of the Christian story was independent of its historical accidents. The importance of the Christian story was that it announced with authority (whether truly or not matters little) that the life of man has significance, a universal significance transcending and including the temporal experience of the individual. This was the secret of its enduring strength, that it irradiated pessimism with hope: it liberated the mind of man from the cycles in which classical philosophy had inclosed it as in a prison, and by transferring the golden age from the past to the future substituted an optimistic for a disillusioned view of human destiny.

The eighteenth-century Philosophers might therefore rewrite the story of man's first state, relegating the Garden of Eden to the limbo of myths; they might discover a new revelation in the book of nature to displace the revelation in Holy Writ; they might demonstrate that reason, supported by the universal assent of mankind as recorded in history, was a more infallible authority than church and state—they might well do all this and yet find their task but half finished. No "return," no "rebirth" of classical philosophy, however idealized and humanized, no worship of ancestors long since dead, or pale imitations of Greek pessimism would suffice for a society that had been so long and so well taught to look forward to another and better world to come. Without a new heaven to replace the old, a new way of salvation, of attaining perfection, the religion of humanity would appeal in vain to the common run of men.

The new heaven had to be located somewhere within the confines of the earthly life, since it was an article of philosophical faith that the end of life is life itself, the perfected temporal life of man; and in the future, since the temporal life was not yet perfected. But if the celestial heaven was to be dismantled in order to be rebuilt on earth, it seemed that the salvation of mankind must be attained, not by some outside, miraculous, catastrophic agency (God or the philosopher-king), but by man himself, by the progressive improvement made by the efforts of successive generations of men; and in this coöperative enterprise posterity had its undeniable uses: posterity would complete what the past and the present had begun. "We have admired our ancestors less," said Chastellux, "but we have loved our contemporaries better, and have expected more of our descendants."[2] Thus, the Philosophers called in posterity to exorcise the double illusion of the Christian paradise and the golden age of antiquity. For the love of God they substituted love of humanity; for the vicarious atonement the perfectibility of man through his own efforts; and for the hope of immortality in another world the hope of living in the memory of future generations.

II

Long before the eighteenth century, writers of high distinction had dimly perceived the services which posterity might one day be called upon to perform. Some day, Seneca said, our posterity will wonder at our ignorance of things which are so clear to them. And Dante, in the high Middle Ages, opened his *De monarchia* with a sentence that implied more perhaps than he would willingly have conceded, that implied in fact all that the eighteenth century had to say on the subject.

All men on whom the Higher Nature has stamped the love of truth should especially concern themselves in laboring for posterity, in order that future generations may be enriched by their efforts, as they themselves were made rich by the efforts of generations past.[3]

[2] *De la félicité publique*, II, 71.
[3] *The De Monarchia of Dante Alighieri*, ed. with translation and notes by Aurelia Henry (1904), Bk. I, chap. i, p. 3.

More than four centuries elapsed before this pregnant idea could play its part in the world. The explanation for this long delay is perhaps not too difficult to find. It could hardly strike Dante's contemporaries as worth while to labor especially for posterity, since the fate of posterity, as of themselves, as of all mankind, had once for all been determined and would presently be pronounced at the judgment day. To Erasmus and his contemporaries the idea, in itself so essentially humane, might have held some special glamor except that it invited them to contemplate the future when they were so fully occupied in admiring the past. The Humanists were far too grateful to the Greeks and Romans for having emancipated them from superstitions to be willing to compare classical civilization unfavorably with their own, still less with that of unknown future generations. They missed the simple fact (and there are still many who refuse to see it) that the true way to imitate the Greeks is not to imitate them, since the Greeks themselves imitated no one. Yet, obviously, a Philosopher could not grasp the modern idea of progress, could not become enamored of posterity, until he was willing to abandon ancestor worship, until he analyzed away his inferiority complex toward the past, and realized that his own generation was superior to any yet known.

Among the pioneers in effecting this reorientation was Francis Bacon. In the *Novum organum* is that famous passage, often quoted, in which he protests against calling the Greeks and Romans ancient: on the contrary, he maintains, they lived in the youth of the world, and it is the moderns who are the true ancients, and who should, for that reason, know more than the Greeks and Romans, having profited by all that has been learned since their time.[4] I do not know whether Pascal had read Bacon or not; but it is certain that he expressed Bacon's idea better than Bacon himself did.

The whole succession of human beings throughout the course of the ages must be regarded as a single man, continually living and learning; and this shows how unwarranted is the deference we yield to the philosophers of antiquity; for, as old age is most distant from infancy, it must be manifest to all that old age in the universal man must be sought, not in the times nearest his birth, but in the times most distant from it. Those whom we call the ancients are really those who lived in the youth of the world, and the true infancy of man; and as we have added the experience of the ages between us and them to what they knew, it is only in ourselves that is to be found that antiquity which we venerate in others.[5]

When Pascal wrote these words the quarrel of the ancients and the moderns was well under way. Professor Bury, in his invaluable book, *The Idea of Progress,* has noted the beginnings of that famous

[4] *Novum organum,* Bk. I, sec. 84.
[5] *Pensées* (1897), II, 271.

polemic. As early as 1620 Allessandro Tassoni speaks of the controversy as already current, and announces himself as, on the whole, on the side of the moderns. In 1627 the English divine George Hakewill published a six-hundred-page book, entitled *An Apologie or Declaration of the Power and Providence of God in the Government of the World,* in which he denied the "common error touching Nature's perpetual and universal decay." The modern world, he maintains, is better than the ancient, so that "the vain shadows of the world's fatal decay" should not "keep us either from looking backward to the imitation of our noble predecessors or forward in providing for posterity, but as our predecessors worthily provided for us, so let our posterity bless us in providing for them." Half a century later Glanvill, defender at once of the doctrines of witchcraft and science (a feat not unknown in our day), maintained that the modern world was far superior to the ancient in the accumulation of useful knowledge, and that it was the duty of present generations to "seek to gather, to observe and examine, and lay up in bank for the ages that are to come."[6] About the same time Desmarets de Saint-Sorlin, who disliked the Greeks (according to Professor Bury, both because he was a fanatical Christian and a bad poet), maintained that the ancient world was neither so learned nor so happy nor so rich and magnificent

[6] *Plus ultra* (1688).

as the modern world, and that Christianity offered better subjects than classical mythology for poets, a fact which he illustrated, not very happily, by writing *Clovis* and *Mary Magdalene*—works which, for some reason, are still less well known than those of Homer and Sophocles.

Sorlin solemnly bequeathed his defense of the moderns to a younger man, Charles Perrault; and the subsequent history of this battle of the books is too well known to need recapitulation here. It may be followed in Perrault's *Parallèle des anciens et des modernes* (1688–96), Fontenelle's *Les anciens et les modernes* (1688); and, for the English record of it, in Sir William Temple's *Essay on Ancient and Modern Learning* (1690), William Wotton's *Reflections upon Ancient and Modern Learning* (1696), and Swift's *Battle of the Books*. It is sufficient to note that the ablest champion of the moderns, Fontenelle, rested his defense upon the Cartesian doctrine of the uniformity of nature. Whether the ancients are superior to the moderns may be settled, Fontenelle says, by asking whether trees were larger in ancient than in modern times: if they were, then a Socrates cannot appear again; if they were not, then he may. Nature is no respecter of ages, and if greatness fails to make its appearance in certain ages—if, for example, the centuries following the barbarian invasions represent a degeneration from classical times—the explanation is not that nature was less potent, but that circumstances were adverse. Such degeneration is not inevitable, but accidental and temporary, a falling away which time will correct. Time is an essential element in the problem, and time is on the side of the angels, that is to say on the side of the moderns, the proof of which may be read in history; for, after centuries of ignorance and superstition, the modern world has recovered ancient learning, emerged from barbarism into a civilized and ordered state, and may very well equal the ancients or even surpass them. It is at this point that Fontenelle advances a step by making a distinction between science and the arts. In poetry and the arts, since these depend on feeling and imagination, the moderns may equal but can scarcely hope to surpass the ancients. But in science and learning, since these depend on knowledge and correct reasoning, later generations must inevitably surpass the ancients for the simple reason that they build upon all the accumulated knowledge of the past. "We are under obligation to the ancients," he says, "for having exhausted almost all the false theories that could be formed."

In supposing that the possibilities of false theories had been exhausted Fontenelle was no doubt oversanguine. To be oversanguine was characteristic of his generation; and if Fontenelle's theories were accepted it was less because of correct reasoning than because the age of Louis XIV was disposed to think well of itself. The Grand Monarch did not readily tolerate invidious comparisons. If it was criminal in the Huguenots to profess another religion than that of the king, it was at least a sign of provincialism in men of letters to suppose that the civilization of Athens could have been superior to that of Versailles. Talleyrand once remarked that those who had not lived before 1789 did not really know how pleasant life could be. Properly qualified, the statement is true enough. During the century that elapsed from Louis XIV to the Revolution, life must have been, for the high-placed favorites of fortune, very pleasant indeed; and never more so than during those quiescent years before 1750, when no king had as yet found it necessary to make witty remarks about the coming deluge. It was an essential part of the smiling complaisance of that contented age, essential to its self-respect, to think of itself as the equal of any yet known.

But if the doctrines of Fontenelle were welcome to his generation, they were also sufficient for it. Fontenelle did, indeed, recognize that future generations would surpass the moderns, since it was evident that in the accumulation and practical application of knowledge "there is no end." Nevertheless, he did not follow up the suggestion: he paid his respects to posterity, but he was in no mood to worship it. Generally speaking, his mood was that of his contemporaries. They were quite content to have abandoned the notion of inevitable degeneration, to have demonstrated that they were not inferior. With the future they were not too much concerned. It was a time to let sleeping dogs lie, a time of quiescence following the religious and political controversies of the seventeenth century, when men were disposed to welcome the theory of Malebranche that God had created as good a world as he could, considering the fact that he had limited himself to working with a few general principles, or even the more thoroughgoing notion of Leibnitz that the world, taking the universe as a whole and in the long run, was the best of possible worlds. The egoism of the age of Walpole and the Regent and the Well Beloved was, therefore, satisfied with the assurance that it need not lament the glory that was Greece, that it could happily sustain comparisons without loss of self-respect, having sufficiently solid, even if somewhat prosaic, glories of its own.

In the later eighteenth century this mood was replaced by another; complaisance gave way to discontent. Optimism remains, is even intensified; but it is no longer an optimism resting on satisfaction with things as they are. It is an optimism projected into the future, sustained by the conviction that what is wrong now will shortly be set right. The conviction that things might be set right without too much difficulty found support in the advancement of science, which more than confirmed Fontenelle's prediction that to the accumulation and practical application of knowledge there was no end; and especially in the psychology of Locke which, reinforced and simplified by Condillac, was generally accepted as self-evident: it was self-evident that man was the product of his environment—of nature and the institutions under which he lived—and that by reshaping his environment in accord with the invariable and determinable laws of nature, his material and spiritual regeneration might be speedily accomplished. The making of a suitable constitution, as they were apt to say in the National Assembly, is a simple matter since it is already engraved on all hearts; is "perhaps . . . but the work of a day, since it is the result of the enlightenment of a century."[7] In the seventeenth century Hakewill had advanced, as one reason for denying the "world's universal decay," the pragmatic argument that such an idea "quails the hopes and blunts the edge of men's endeavours." It is in the later eighteenth century that we can verify the reverse of this idea, namely, that when men hope much and greatly endeavor they are eager to believe in the world's speedy and universal amelioration. The determination to set things right, which culminated in the great Revolution, generated and sustained and gave an emotional and even a religious quality to the conviction that the future—the immediate future it

[7] Barère, *Archives parlementaires*, VIII, 231.

might very well be—would be infinitely better than the present or the past.

It was more especially in France, where social discontent was most acute, that the doctrine of progress, of perfectibility, became an essential article of faith in the new religion of humanity. Fontenelle had thought of progress in terms of the gradual increase in knowledge and correct reasoning. It did not occur to him, or to many of his contemporaries, to look forward to any radical regeneration of morals or of social institutions. To play with the idea of utopia, as described by Plato or Thomas More or Bacon, was an engaging pastime no doubt; to project it, as something to be practically realized, into the future history of France, would have seemed to him scarcely less an illusion than the naïve dream of perfection in the Garden of Eden. Yet this is just what, under the pressure of social discontents, came to pass: the utopian dream of perfection, that necessary compensation for the limitations and frustrations of the present state, having been long identified with the golden age or the Garden of Eden or life eternal in the Heavenly City of God, and then by the sophisticated transferred to remote or imagined lands (the moon or Atlantis or Nowhere, Tahiti or Pennsylvania or Peking), was at last projected into the life of man on earth and identified with the desired and hoped-for regeneration of society.

This transformation of the old utopian dream may

be followed in the writings of the Philosophers: not alone in those well-known formal treatises on the subject of progress—Turgot's discourses, Lessing's *Education of the Human Race,* Herder's *Ideas on the Philosophy of the History of Mankind,* Condorcet's *Sketch of the Progress of the Human Spirit;* but equally well in the writings of other Philosophers, in writings not immediately concerned with that subject. The Philosophers were, almost without exception, much concerned with progress, perfectibility, the fate of posterity; and this interest, needless to say, was intimately associated with their interest in history. The past, the present, and the future state of mankind were for them but aspects of the same preoccupation. The Philosophers were, after all, primarily concerned with the present state of things, which they wished to change; and they needed good reasons for their desire to change it. They wished to justify their discontents, to validate their aversions; and they accomplished this object by enlarging the social specious present, by projecting the present state into the centuries, where it could be seen to be but a passing unhappy phase of the universal experience of mankind.

III

In this enterprise posterity played an important rôle: it replaced God as judge and justifier of those virtuous and enlightened ones who were not of this world. All men in some degree need outside approval for what they think and do—the approval of loved ones, of kith and kin, of the community of right-minded men. Most men in all times obtain the required approval by following the established customs and professing the common opinions. But there are always some eccentric individuals, and on occasion certain groups, who find the present temporal world of men and things intolerable. So they withdraw from it, living in spiritual exile, or else they endeavor to transform it. In either case they are likely to lose the approval of the community, and losing the approval of the community they seek the approval of some power above or beyond it, of some authority more universally valid than that of the present world of men and things: they seek the approval of God, or the law of nature, or the inevitable class conflict, or the force outside themselves that makes for righteousness. The isolated ones, like Archimedes, find that without a fulcrum upon which to rest their lever they cannot move the inert and resistant world of men and things as they are. The eighteenth-century revolutionists, whether in thought or in deed, responded to this need. Finding themselves out of harmony with the temporary world of men and things, they endeavored to put themselves in tune with the infinite powers: over against the ephemeral customs and mores, they set the universal laws of nature and of nature's God; from the immediate judgments of men, they appealed to the universal judgment of humanity. Humanity was an abstraction, no doubt; but through the beneficent law of progress the wisdom of the ages would be accumulated, transmitted, and placed at the disposal of posterity. Every age would be the posterity of all preceding ages; and as the eighteenth century, in the light of two thousand years of human experience, had vindicated Socrates and Regulus against the erring opinion of their times, so generations yet to come would vindicate the Voltaires and the Rousseaus, the Robespierres and the Rolands.

I do not know why historians, who are ardently devoted to noting exactly what happened, should so generally have failed to note a fact that is writ large in the most authentic documents: the fact that the thought of posterity was apt to elicit from eighteenth-century Philosophers and revolutionary leaders a highly emotional, an essentially religious, response. Posterity, like nature, was often personified, reverently addressed as a divinity, and invoked in the accents of prayer. This, too, is a fact to be recorded, as curious and interesting as many another on which historians have lavished their erudition. I take at random an example of this phenomenon. Robespierre is speaking before the Jacobin Club on the question of war with Austria, and he ends his speech with the following invocation:

O posterity, sweet and tender hope of humanity, thou

art not a stranger to us; it is for thee that we brave all the blows of tyranny; it is thy happiness which is the price of our painful struggles: often discouraged by the obstacles that surround us, we feel the need of thy consolations; it is to thee that we confide the task of completing our labors, and the destiny of all the unborn generations of men! . . . May the martyrs of liberty occupy in thy memory the place which the heroes of imposture and aristocracy have usurped in ours; . . . may thy first impulse be to scorn traitors and hate tyrants; may thy motto be: protection, love, benevolence to the unhappy, eternal war to oppressors! Make haste, O posterity, to bring to pass the hour of equality, of justice, of happiness![8]

This perfervid invocation makes us smile no doubt; but do the opponents of Robespierre meet it with derision? No, indeed. They do not blaspheme. Louvet replies:

Robespierre, . . . your speeches belong to posterity, and posterity will come to judge between you and me, but meantime you assume the gravest responsibility. In persisting in your opinion you are under obligation to your contemporaries, and even to posterity. Yes, posterity will come to judge between you and me. Unworthy as I may be, she will say that a man appeared in the National Assembly untouched by all the passions of the time; one of the most faithful of the tribunes of the people, it is neces-

[8] C. Vellay, *Discours et rapports de Robespierre* (1908), p. 155. Cf. *Journal des débats de la société des amis de la constitution* (January, 1792), No. 127, p. 3.

sary to esteem and cherish his virtues, admire his courage, . . .[9]

Robespierre and Louvet are fully aware that there is to be a judgment day in which virtue will be vindicated and corruption condemned, but in their theology posterity has elbowed God out of the judgment seat: it is posterity that will judge and justify and award the immortal crown.

Men rarely love humanity more fervently than when they are engaged in deadly conflict with each other, and it is true that the prestige of posterity was never quite so high as during the crucial months of the Revolution. Nevertheless, the Philosophers, and not French Philosophers only, were well aware of the uses of posterity long before 1789. Priestley, for example, a quite sane and sound Englishman, in his treatise on government, turns aside from the main theme to tell us what an inspiration it was to contemplate "the progress of the species towards perfection." In a state of society,

it requires but a few years to comprehend the whole preceding progress of any one art or science; and the rest of a man's life, in which his faculties are the most perfect, may be given to the extension of it. If, by this means, one art or science should grow too large for an easy comprehension, . . . a commodious subdivision will be made. Thus all knowledge will be subdivided and extended; and

[9] *Journal des débats de la société des amis de la constitution* (January, 1792), No. 134; Débats, No. 130, p. 4.

knowledge, as Lord Bacon observes, being *power,* the human powers will, in fact, be enlarged; nature, including both its materials, and its laws, will be more at our command; men will make their situation in this world abundantly more easy and comfortable; they will probably prolong their existence in it, and will grow daily more happy, each in himself, and more able (and, I believe, more disposed) to communicate happiness to others. Thus, whatever was the beginning of this world, the end will be glorious and paradisaical, beyond what our imagi[n]ations can now conceive. Extravagant as some may suppose these views to be, I think I could show them to be fairly suggested by the true theory of human nature, and to arise from the natural course of human affairs. But, for the present, I waive this subject, the contemplation of which always makes me happy.[10]

Herder would not have thought Priestley's views extravagant. His great work on the philosophy of history, strange compound of learning, insight, and mystical piety, is scarcely more than an elaboration of Priestley's thesis, a sustained oratorical exposition of the text that God realizes himself in humanity, and that all good men, in working for the happiness of posterity, are furthering the divine purpose, and may here and now anticipate the heavenly reward. In a passage not infrequently quoted, he says:

It is a beautiful dream of future life to think of oneself

[10] *An Essay on the First Principles of Government; and on the Nature of Political, Civil, and Religious Liberty* (1771), pp. 4–5.

in friendly converse with all the wise and good who have ever worked for mankind, and have entered that higher realm with the sweet reward of labor accomplished; but in a sense history already opens to us this pleasant bower of speech and association with the upright and right-thinking men of many times. Here Plato stands before me; there I hear Socrates' friendly questions and share with him his final fate. If Marcus Aurelius speaks in communion with his own heart he speaks also to mine, and poor Epictetus gives commands more potent than those of a king. The perplexed Tully, the unfortunate Boethius speak to me, communicate to me the circumstances of their lives, the grief and the consolation of their souls. . . . Manifold is the problem of humanity, and everywhere the result of human striving this: "Upon reason and integrity depends the essence of our race, its end and its fate." No nobler use has history than this: it leads us as it were into the council of fate and teaches us to conform to the eternal laws of nature. While it shows us the defects and consequences of all unreason, it teaches us our place in that great organism in which reason and goodness struggle with chaotic forces, always however according to their nature creating order, and pressing forward on the path of victory.[11]

In Herder we hear the Philosophers' Manifesto, calling upon virtuous men of all countries and all ages to unite against evil and unreason. They will find their reward in heaven, no doubt, but also in the favorable judgment of posterity.

[11] *Sämmtliche Werke* (1877–1913), XIV, 251–252.

Of all the Philosophers perhaps none ever gave so much thought to the uses of posterity as Diderot—Diderot, in whose mind all the intellectual currents of the age crossed and went their separate ways. One evening in the year 1765, so we are told, Diderot and Falconet, "in a corner by the fire, in the Rue Taranne, argued the question whether a regard for posterity inspired men to noble action and the creation of great works."[12] It seems that Falconet had propounded one of those conundrums, of the prize essay species, so dear to the curious and argumentative mind of the century. Assuming it could be proved that at a certain date, not too far in the future, a comet would collide with the earth and totally destroy it—what effect would this knowledge have on the conduct of men? None at all, Falconet maintained. On the contrary, a most disastrous effect, Diderot replied: such knowledge would destroy all incentive to good or great action. "No more ambition, no more monuments, poets, historians, perhaps no more warriors or wars. Everyone would cultivate his garden and plant his cabbages."[13] So arguing, the two men separated for the night; but the question would not down, and presently they were discussing it in an exchange of letters. The correspondence ran for some years, and the letters of Diderot alone, some of which are veritable pamphlets, fill more than

[12] Diderot, *Oeuvres,* XVIII, 79.
[13] *Ibid.,* IX, 435, 436.

two hundred pages of his collected works.[14] More than two hundred pages of frantic writing chiefly devoted to proving that if it were certainly known that the world would come to an end, if it were known that there would be no posterity to reward and punish, men would straightway rush into evil courses!

Falconet took the question lightly enough, too lightly for Diderot's taste; but Diderot himself took it in deadly earnest. All his life it worried him, and he worried it, so that again and again we find him making some new and tempestuous assault upon it—in *Le neveu de Rameau,* in the *Physiology,* in the *Essay on Claudius and Nero.* What concerned Diderot was the old insoluble question of the foundations of morality and the good life. The old foundations of morality and the good life (faith in God and the life after death) Diderot's intelligence had analyzed away. But if there was no heavenly reward after death, what was left? Why should any man deny himself? Why suffer persecution for truth and justice without compensation here or hereafter? Whatever Diderot's intellect might say, the good heart of the man assured him that virtue was the most certain of realities; and since it was a reality there must be

[14] For the letters of Diderot to Falconet on this subject, see Diderot, *Oeuvres,* XVIII, 79–336. Étienne Maurice Falconet was a noted sculptor of his time and professor in the Royal Academy of Painting and Sculpture. His letters to Diderot are known chiefly through the quotations made by Diderot in his replies. But see *Gazette des beaux arts,* Second Period, II, 129–135.

compensation for the practice of it. The only compensation Diderot could ever find was the hope of living forever in the memory of posterity. "Do you not see," he exclaims, "that the judgment of posterity anticipated is the sole encouragement, the sole support, the sole consolation . . . of men in a thousand unhappy circumstances?"[15] "If our predecessors have done nothing for us, and if we do nothing for our descendants, it is almost in vain that nature wills that man should be perfectible."[16] "All these philosophers, these men of integrity who have been the victims of stupid people, of atrocious priests, of enraged tyrants, what consolation remains to them in the hour of death? This: that prejudice passes, and that posterity will transfer to their enemies the ignominy which they have suffered."[17] It is significant that throughout this discussion Diderot employs the phrases "sentiment of immortality" and "respect for posterity." The "sentiment of immortality and respect for posterity move the heart and elevate the soul; they are two germs of great things, two promises as substantial as any others." The ideas, the phrases, are essentially religious, essentially Christian: for the worship of God, Diderot has substituted respect for posterity; for the hope of immortality in heaven, the hope of living in the memory of future generations. And in the very accents of a Christian

[15] *Oeuvres*, XVIII, 102.   [16] *Ibid.*, p. 179.
[17] *Ibid.*, p. 100.

priest he can invoke his divinity. "O Posterity, holy and sacred! Support of the oppressed and unhappy, thou who art just, thou who art uncorruptible, thou who wilt revenge the good man and unmask the hypocrite, consoling and certain idea, do not abandon me!" The essence of the matter Diderot managed to reduce to an epigram: "Posterity is for the Philosopher what the other world is for the religious."[18]

Diderot would have understood Robespierre's invocation to posterity; he would have understood Louvet's appeal to posterity for judgment. He would have understood the Girondists and Jacobins, those representatives of Latium and the Peloponnesus, ostentatiously draping themselves in Roman virtues lest posterity should fail to recognize and reward them. He would have understood Condorcet. It has been noted as remarkable that Condorcet, proscribed and in hiding, with all his high revolutionary hopes fallen about him, should have persevered in the faith sufficiently to write his famous sketch of the progress of the human spirit. But no: never did he so much need the consolation of believing in the perfectibility of the human race as when death stared him in the face. Then it was that the vision of posterity,

freed from its chains, . . . marching with sure steps on the road to truth, virtue, and happiness, consoles the philosopher for the errors, the crimes, the injustices that still soil the earth, and of which he himself is often the victim.

[18] *Oeuvres*, XVIII, 101.

It is in the contemplation of this picture . . . that he finds his true recompense for virtue. The contemplation of this picture is an asylum in which the memory of his persecutors does not follow him, an asylum in which, living in imagination with mankind re-established in its rights and in its true nature, he can forget mankind corrupted and tormented by greed, fear, envy. It is in this asylum that he truly lives with his fellows, in a *heaven* which his reason has created, and which his love of humanity embellishes with the purest joys.[19]

And that still more famous Girondist, Madame Roland: I suppose no one ever professed the religion of humanity with more unquestioned faith, practiced it more assiduously, or in the end found its consolations more genuine and sustaining. The stuffy apartment of an engraver doing a small business on the Pont Neuf was no adequate theater for displaying the talents of a young woman who communed familiarly with the saints and sages of the world, and who never "read of a single act of courage or of virtue" without feeling herself capable of imitating it under similar circumstances. She often wept to think she was not born a Spartan or a Roman, well knowing that had she been Socrates she would have drunk the hemlock, had she been Regulus she too would have returned to Carthage. Since neither opportunity was likely to come to her on the Pont Neuf, she "per-

[19] *Esquisse d'un tableau historique des progrès de l'esprit humain* (1797), pp. 293–294.

suaded herself that she ought to be busy in perfecting her own being." Yet where could this perfected being move and speak and act the part? Where could she converse with those who would understand her, where do heroic deeds or make sacrifices that would not go unrewarded or unacclaimed? Not in the real world of Paris, but in the world of history, in the world of Plutarch and Jean Jacques, in the world of the imagination: there was a world in which others might see her as she saw herself.

In this world of the imagination the real Madame Roland, that perfected being which Madame Roland had created, lived until the Revolution quite unexpectedly, quite miraculously so it seemed, offered her an opportunity to play a noble rôle in the actual world of affairs. A few brief months as it proved, and then proscription: the poor lady sits in prison, waiting the end. Then she remembers that martyrdom has always been the fate of martyrs: recalls the "death of Socrates, the exile of Aristides, the condemnation of Phocion"; is aware all at once that heaven has destined her "to be a witness to crimes similar to those of which they were the victims, and to participate in the glory of a persecution of the same kind." Sitting in prison she therefore wrote her memoirs, for "what better can one do in prison than to transport one's existence elsewhere by a happy fiction or interesting memories?" What, indeed!

Seen too closely, her brief adventure in revolution was a failure and her death meaningless. But transported elsewhere, projected into history and looked at from the perspective of the centuries, both her life and her death could be regarded as in some sense the work of a higher power—of God, or the associated fates, or whatever beneficent forces might be supposed to concern themselves with human destiny. So regarded, her whole life unrolled before her, in recollection, as a miraculous preparation for the final sacrifice on the altar of human liberty. Where, then, was the sting of death when it could be regarded as predestined, as an event of more than personal or local significance, an event which coming generations might be disposed to record in humanity's great book of martyrdoms? Posterity, she was persuaded, would so regard it. "Roland will never die in posterity, and I also, I shall have some measure of existence in future generations." Her memoirs she entitled, *An Impartial Appeal to Posterity,* and Bosc, who edited them, tells us that "Citoyenne Roland endeavored to find in the esteem of posterity the means of consoling herself for the injustice of contemporaries, and in future glory compensation for her anticipated death." Posterity was for Madame Roland, as for Diderot, what the other world was for the religious: sustained, like the Christian martyrs of an earlier time, by the hope of immortality, she could mount the scaffold with courage and lift unflinching eyes to the poised and relentless knife.[20]

IV

Nearly a century ago De Tocqueville noted the fact that the French Revolution was a "political revolution which functioned in the manner and which took on in some sense the aspect of a religious revolution." Like Islamism or the Protestant revolt, it overflowed the frontiers of countries and nations and was extended by "preaching and propaganda." It functioned,

in relation to this world, in precisely the same manner that religious revolutions function in respect to the other: it considered the citizen in an abstract fashion, apart from particular societies, in the same way that religions consider man in general, independently of time and place. It sought not merely the particular rights of French citizens, but the general political rights and duties of all men. [Accordingly] since it appeared to be more concerned with the regeneration of the human race than with the reformation of France, it generated a passion which, until then, the most violent political revolutions had never exhibited. It inspired proselytism and gave birth to propaganda. It could therefore assume that appearance of a religious revolution which so astonished contemporaries; or rather it became itself a kind of new

[20] For an elaboration of what is here said about Madame Roland, see *American Historical Review*, XXXIII, 784.

religion, an imperfect religion it is true, a religion without God, without a form of worship, and without a future life, but one which nevertheless, like Islamism, inundated the earth with soldiers, apostles, and martyrs.[21]

De Tocqueville's contemporaries were too much preoccupied with political issues and the validity of traditional religious doctrines to grasp the significance of his pregnant observations. Not until our own time have historians been sufficiently detached from religions to understand that the Revolution, in its later stages especially, took on the character of a religious crusade. But it is now well understood (thanks to the writings of Mathiez, Aulard, and many lesser historians), not only that the Revolution attempted to substitute the eighteenth-century religion of humanity for the traditional faiths, but also that, contrary to the belief of De Tocqueville, the new religion was *not* without God, forms of worship, or a future life. On the contrary, the new religion had its dogmas, the sacred principles of the Revolution—*Liberté et sainte égalité*. It had its form of worship, an adaptation of Catholic ceremonial, which was elaborated in connection with the civic *fêtes*. It had its saints, the heroes and martyrs of liberty. It was sustained by an emotional impulse, a mystical faith in humanity, in the ultimate regeneration of the human race. While Louis was still on

[21] *L'ancien régime et la Révolution,* Bk. I, chap. iii.

his throne contemporaries (knowing their Rousseau) recognized that

a religion which made the fatherland and the laws the object of *adoration* for all citizens would be in the eyes of a wise man an excellent religion. Its Pontiff would be the king, the supreme ruler. To die for the fatherland would be to achieve eternal glory, eternal happiness. The man who violated the laws of his country would be impious, and the first magistrate, king and Pontiff, would rightly give him over to public execration, in the name of the society which he had offended, and in the name of the divinity who has placed us all equally under the restraint of impartial laws.[22]

The civic *fêtes*, beginning with the first celebration (July 14, 1790) of the taking of the Bastille, the dechristianization movement, and the Festival of Reason in November, 1793, were tentative, preliminary stages in the effort to substitute for the Christian religion a civic and, as one may say, secular religion of humanity. The Festival of November is commonly called the Festival of Reason, and it has been pointed out that it was somewhat unfortunate to choose an actress to represent that cold abstraction. In truth it was Liberty, not Reason, that the festival was intended to honor: the actress represented Liberty, the torch represented Reason enlightening Liberty. The intention was perfectly ex-

[22] Nicolas de Bonneville, *De l'esprit des religions* (1791), Part II, 39.

pressed by the hymn, composed for the occasion by Marie-Joseph Chénier, which was chanted in the de-christianized Cathedral of Notre Dame:

> Descend, O Liberty, daughter of Nature;
> The people, recovering thy immortal power,
> Upon the stately ruins of old imposture,
>   Raise once again thy altar!
>
> Come, conqueror of kings, Europe's example;
> Come, over false Gods complete thy success!
> Thou, Saint Liberty, inhabit this temple,
>   Be of our nation the Goddess![23]

The Festival of November was nevertheless thought to be, for reasons into which we need not stop to inquire, too "atheistical," and atheism, as Robespierre explained, was aristocratic. The final form assumed by the new religion during the Revolution was fixed by the decree of May, 1794, on the Worship of the Supreme Being:

> The French people recognize the existence of the Supreme Being and the immortality of the soul.—It recognizes that the worship worthy of the Supreme Being is the practice of the duties of man.—It places in the front rank of these duties to detest bad faith and tyranny, to punish tyrants and traitors, to aid the unfortunate, to respect the weak, to defend the oppressed, to do unto others all possible good and to be unjust to no one.—There shall be

[23] Aulard, *Le culte de la raison*, p. 54; *Oeuvres de M. J. Chénier* (1824), III, 357.

instituted fêtes in order to remind man of the Divinity and of the dignity of his being.—These fêtes shall take their names from the glorious events of our Revolution, the virtues most cherished and most useful to man, and the great gifts of nature.—The French Republic shall annually celebrate the fêtes of the 14th July, 1789, the 10th August, 1792, the 21st January, 1793, and the 31st May, 1793.—It shall celebrate every tenth day the fêtes which are hereby enumerated.[24]

Among the thirty-six *fêtes* of the *decadi* it was inevitable that there should be included *fêtes* in honor of liberty and equality, love of the fatherland, hatred of tyrants, frugality, stoicism, agriculture, and posterity.

After the great Revolution had spent its fury, faith in the new religion of humanity lost much of its mystic and perfervid quality. Still it lived on, inspiring, in the new world and in the old, many lesser revolutions; and it had even one great revival before and during the splendid debacle of 1848. Some there were for whom, even in defeat, it never quite lost its glamor and high promise. Mazzini was their prophet. Of the persistence of the faith unimpaired among obscure men, Gabriel Monod has preserved for us a striking example.

About forty years ago a good woman, who kept the boarding house where I took my meals, related to me an

[24] Aulard, *Le culte de la raison,* p. 273.

anecdote about her father, a simple workingman of Nantes, which greatly impressed me. This man was very young when the Revolution broke out. He accepted it with enthusiasm; took part in the struggle of the Jacobins against the Vendéeans; witnessed with regret the imperial *régime* destroy the democratic liberties so dearly bought; and at each revolution, in 1814, in 1830, in 1848, believed that the ideal republic, dreamed of in 1793, was about to be reborn. He died during the second Empire, more than ninety years old, and at the moment of death, raising to heaven a look of ecstasy, was heard to murmur: "O sun of '93, I shall die at last without having seen thy rays again." This man, like the first Christians, lived in the hope of the millennium.[25]

The anecdote doubtless lost nothing in the telling. Yet it serves well enough to symbolize the fact that the eighteenth-century religion of humanity accompanied and sustained the political and social revolution which was gradually accomplished, with whatever concessions in theory, with whatever compromises in practice, during the hundred years that followed the taking of the Bastille. The concessions and the compromises were indeed many and flagrant. Madame Roland would have mounted the scaffold with less assurance could she have foreseen the third French Republic, that shabby substitute for the ideal, established in default by monarchists, a republic without a constitution properly speaking,

[25] Mathiez, *Contributions à l'histoire religieuse de la Révolution française*, preface by Monod, p. i.

without a declaration of the imprescriptible rights of man. Mazzini, as we know, could never quite believe in the validity of that Italian freedom which Cavour achieved by diplomatic intrigue and war, and with the aid of Napoleon III, the man who had set his heel on liberty in France. As for Germany, the right to make speeches and resolutions in the *Reichstag* was won, not by the speeches and resolutions of the Frankfurt Assembly of '48, but by "blood and iron," by Bismarck, the man who, having no faith in democracy, conceded universal suffrage as a "species of political blackmail," a necessary move in the game. The German Empire, the third French Republic, the Kingdom of Italy, the Austro-Hungarian "Compromise," a "household suffrage" thrown as a sop to tenants on entailed estates—these, and similar tarnished imitations, were the "rewards" which posterity, after a century of enlightenment, grudgingly bestowed upon the impassioned propagandists and martyrs of the democratic faith. The great Revolution, as an accomplished fact, betrayed the hopes of its prophets, the Rousseaus and the Condorcets, the Robespierres and the Rolands, the Mazzinis and the Kossuths. No doubt the illusion of its prophets was to suppose that the evil propensities of men would disappear with the traditional forms through which they functioned. Before the end of the nineteenth century, at all events, it was obvious that the abolition of old oppressions and inequities had done little

160

more than make room for new ones; and when men
realized that democratic government as a reality, as
it actually functioned in that besmirched age of iron,
was, after all, only another way of being indifferently
governed, those once glamorous words, *liberté, égalité, fraternité,* lost their prophetic power for the
contented, and the eighteenth-century religion of humanity, suffering the fate of all successful religions,
fell to the level of a conventional and perfunctory
creed for the many.

Meantime, the discontented were renouncing the
democratic faith to follow the prophets of a new religion. "Working men of all countries, unite!" In the
Communist Manifesto, Karl Marx and Friederich
Engels sounded the battle cry of a new social religion. Like the eighteenth-century religion of humanity, the communist faith was founded on the laws of
nature as revealed by science. But science had made
advances since the eighteenth century. In the eighteenth century, nature was regarded as a delicately
adjusted machine, a stationary engine whose mecha-
nism implied the existence of a purposeful engineer,
a beneficent first cause or Author of the Universe.
With Hegel the beneficent Author of the Universe
faded away into a diaphanous Transcendent Idea,
and with Darwin the Transcendent Idea disappeared
altogether. Henceforth, God, and all the substitutes
for that conception, could be ignored since nature
was conceived not as a finished machine but as an

unfinished process, a mechanistic process, indeed, but one generating its own power. Supplied with the dialectic of Hegel and the evolutionary theories of Darwin, Marx formulated, in *Das Kapital*, the creed of the communist faith which was to replace, for the discontented, the democratic faith of the eighteenth century. The new faith, like the old, looks to the past and to the future; like the old, it sees in the past a persistent conflict, and in the future a millennial state. But the new faith is less anthropomorphic, less personal than the old. It does not look back to a golden age or a Garden of Eden. It does not see in the history of mankind the deliberate and sinister betrayal of good men by the evil-minded. It does not look forward to the regeneration of humanity by the pleasant specific of enlightenment and good will. It sees in the past a ruthless and impersonal conflict of material forces; a conflict functioning through the economic class interests of men, which, as it created the landowning aristocratic *régime* of the Middle Ages and then destroyed it in the interest of the *bourgeois*-capitalist *régime* of the nineteenth century, will in turn destroy the *bourgeois*-capitalist *régime* in the interest of the proletariat. The social revolution, conceived as the collapse of the capitalist *régime,* is coming, not through enlightenment and the preaching of good will, but through the indefeasible operation of economic forces. The function of intelligence is to understand these forces; the duty of common men is to adjust themselves, in the light of intelligence, to the inevitable process. The stars in their courses, rather than the puny will of man, will bring about the social revolution, a kind of promised land to which the masses may look forward with faith and hope.

And now, in our day, the first act in the social revolution, accompanied and sustained by the communist faith, has just been staged in Russia. Between the Russian and the French revolutions, as between the democratic and the communist faiths, there are no doubt many points of difference; but what concerns us is that the differences, in the long view, are probably superficial, while the similarities are fundamental. If we, the beneficiaries of the French Revolution, fail to note the similarities, it is because we are easily deceived by a slight difference in nomenclature (for "people" read "proletariat," for "aristocrats" read *"bourgeoisie,"* for "kings" read "capitalist government"); and we are more than willing to be deceived because we, the beneficiaries of the French Revolution, would be the dispossessed of the Russian Revolution should it be successful throughout the western world. Like Diderot's Rameau, we are disposed, naturally enough, to think, "The devil take the best of possible worlds if I am not a part of it." But whatever we think, the plain fact is that the Russian Revolution which menaces us, like the French Revolution which destroyed the possessing classes of the *Old Régime* that we might succeed them, is being carried through in behalf of the dispossessed classes. It aims at nothing less than the establishment of liberty and equality ("true liberty and equality" this time, of course) in place of tyranny and exploitation. For the accomplishment of this object it employs, deliberately, as a temporary but necessary measure, a dictatorship of the faithful similar to that which functioned in '93. And the Bolsheviks who control the Council of Commissars, like the Jacobins who controlled the Committee of Safety, regard themselves as the fated instruments of a process which will inevitably, in the long run, break down the factitious division between nations by uniting all the oppressed against all oppressors. "If cabinets unite kings against the people," exclaimed Isnard in 1792, "we will unite peoples against kings." Similarly, the Bolshevik leaders, following Karl Marx, call upon the "proletarians of all countries" to unite against all *bourgeois*-capitalist governments. The Russian is most of all like the French Revolution in this, that its leaders, having received the tablets of eternal law, regard the "revolution" not merely as an instrument of political and social reform but much more as the realization of a philosophy of life which being universally valid because it is in harmony with science and history must prevail. For this reason the Russian Revolution like the French Revolution has its dogmas, its ceremonial, its saints. Its dogmas are the theories of Marx interpreted by Lenin. The days which it celebrates are the great days of the Revolution. Its saints are the heroes and martyrs of the communist faith. In the homes of the faithful the portrait of Lenin replaces the sacred icons of the old religion, and every day the humble builders of a new order make pilgrimages to his tomb as formerly they made pilgrimages to holy places.

Another resemblance there is: In the minds, or rather in the *breasts* of its enemies, the Russian Revolution arouses the same unreasoning, emotional revulsion which formerly the French Revolution aroused in the breasts of the counter-revolutionists. This emotional revulsion, compounded of fear and anger, was then, as it is now, automatically stimulated by the sound of certain words. To the Castlereaghs and Metternichs of 1815 the words "revolution," "Jacobinism," "republicanism," were suffused with a sense of universal and unconditioned evil realizing itself in certain concrete events. The "revolution" meant the French Revolution of 1789, but it was also, for that very reason, a symbol of universal revolution, of universal denial, *der Geist der stets Verneint:* "the revolution" meant quite simply anarchy in government and atheism in religion. "The revolution" was "Jacobinism," and Jacobinism was "republicanism"; and it was not to be doubted that the visionary ideas which these words expressed, ideas which for twenty-five years had proved their futility by turning Europe upside down, were a menace to established order, to peace and prosperity, to the welfare of mankind. To the Castlereaghs and Metternichs of our day the word "Bolshevism" is the symbol of all that is horrendously antisocial, just as the word "Jacobinism" was to the Castlereaghs and Metternichs of 1815; and the words "soviet" and "communism" have for the beneficiaries of modern democracy the same ominous import that the word "republicanism" formerly had for the beneficiaries of the age of kings and nobles.

The Castlereaghs and the Metternichs of 1815 would have been dismayed indeed to know that before the end of the century the anarchic and atheistical doctrines of the Jacobin faith would undermine the established order throughout the western world. The Castlereaghs and the Metternichs of our time, and even lesser people like ourselves, are permitted to wonder what the next hundred years will bring forth. Will the new religion (call it a religion of humanity or of inhumanity as you like) make its way, however gradually, against whatever opposition, by whatever concessions and compromises, with whatever abatement of fanaticism and ruthlessness, and become in its turn the accepted and the conventional faith? It is possible. A hundred years is a long time, and even now, in the very stronghold of "capitalism," we hear much talk of the "breakdown ' of the competitive system, many suggestions, timid and tentative though they may be, that imply the necessity of regulation. A new word has recently made its entrance, very unobtrusively—"planning." Nothing very radical has as yet been suggested, nor has much been done, in that way. It has been suggested by a high official that every third row of cotton be plowed under, and in certain states governors have called out the military in order to regulate the production of oil. In the way of constructive planning this is not much. But so much talk, and even any slight action by those in high places, indicates at least a certain awareness that what is needed in our high-powered technological society is less liberty and more control, a less freely competitive and a more consciously regulated economy.

A hundred years is a long time, and it is possible that within a hundred years a regulated economy (call it communism or collective planning as you like) may be recognized throughout the western world as the indispensable foundation of social order, peace and prosperity, the welfare of mankind. If that should by any chance be what fortune has in store for us, it is not too fanciful to suppose that "posterity," in the year 2032, will be celebrating the events of November, 1917, as a happy turning point in the history of human freedom, much as we celebrate the events of July, 1789. What, then, are we to think of all these "great days," these intimations of

167

utopia? Are we to suppose that the Russian Revolution of the twentieth century, like the French Revolution of the eighteenth, is but another stage in the progress of mankind toward perfection? Or should we think, with Marcus Aurelius, that "the man of forty years, if he have a grain of sense, in view of this sameness has seen all that has been and shall be"?